Miracle

Miracle

The extraordinary dog
that refused to die

Amanda Leask

EBURY
PRESS

3 5 7 9 10 8 6 4 2

Ebury Press, an imprint of Ebury Publishing
20 Vauxhall Bridge Road
London SW1V 2SA

Ebury Press is part of the Penguin Random House group of companies
whose addresses can be found at global.penguinrandomhouse.com

Penguin
Random House
UK

The author has recreated events, locales and conversations from
her memories of them. In order to maintain the anonymity of some
characters in some instances, the author has changed
some identifying characteristics and details.

June Burden's poems, 'Unity', 'Miracle' and 'The Journey'
used with her explicit permission © June Burden 2015

Amanda Leask has asserted her right to be identified as the author of this
Work in accordance with the Copyright, Designs and Patents Act 1988

First published by Ebury Press in 2016

www.eburypublishing.co.uk

A CIP catalogue record for this book is available from the British Library

Hardback ISBN 9781785032554

Typeset in India by Thomson Digital Pvt Ltd, Noida, Delhi

Printed and bound in Great Britain by Clays Ltd, St Ives PLC

MIX
Paper from
responsible sources
FSC
www.fsc.org   FSC® C018179

Penguin Random House is committed to
a sustainable future for our business, our
readers and our planet. This book is made from
Forest Stewardship Council® certified paper.

To Kyle and Ty – together, we breathed for 29 weeks

Ty's hand and footprint, taken just after birth

Contents

Contents

Kyle's fingerprint and Miracle's paw print

Crufts 2015

It had been a bright spring day in Birmingham, cold but uplifting. The city was abuzz with visitors; more than usual because it was Crufts weekend, the few days when the National Exhibition Centre welcomes tens of thousands of dog lovers to an event that has become a British institution.

I had been there many times in the past with my dogs, showing them eagerly and always waiting with bated breath to see if we would be one of the best. Today, however, was very different. This was the day my life would change forever. It wasn't for the first time, but I truly believe that something happened that day which will have repercussions for many people and many animals across the world for longer than I'll be around. We are all here for such a little while – all we can hope is that we will leave the world a better place, but sometimes we need a helping hand to do that . . . or a helping paw.

As I stood on a brightly-lit stage at Crufts with my beautiful dog and my wonderful son beside me, the cheering and applause of thousands filled the air. Camera flashes were going off from every angle and there was such a sense of joy. I was so happy and so proud – my stunning white rescue dog, Miracle, and my gorgeous 6-year-old son Kyle, had just won the Eukanuba 'Friends for Life' award.

Neither Miracle nor Kyle had been given an easy path in life. They were both fighters, both souls who were locked in their own pasts of pain and heartache. But they had found each other; and in doing so, they weren't just changing their own lives, they were changing the lives of so many more. Standing beside them, I felt immensely proud of what we had achieved, us Three Musketeers, always together, fighting every day. Each of us – Mum, boy, dog – were like individual parts of the same puzzle who, when joined together, could achieve so much more. It was wonderful to think of how far we had come in such a short time.

Around us at the event were people who make dogs their world, people who recognise just what they consider represents a perfect example of a breed. They know what is the best coat or the best tail, they know how ears should stand or flop, how curly or straight fur ought to be, whether a certain colour is more acceptable than another colour – and all the dogs are beautiful. But I knew what made a perfect pair of friends, and they were both beside me.

I was bursting with happiness but I also knew that, much as my two boys deserved this, no one knew the full story of what had brought them together. Two broken souls, both trapped inside themselves with no way to let the world know what they had been through or what still caused them upset, Kyle and Miracle were made for each other.

As I reflected on how little the world really knew of what their pasts had been, my heart raced and that voice, that little voice we all have in our heads that encourages us and wills us on, got louder and louder.

So, tell them then, it said, *tell the world*.

Throughout that evening and the days which followed, the voice got louder and I started listening harder. *Tell them; tell the world*, I heard over and over again. Eventually I listened, eventually I gave in.

So I decided – that's just what I'm going to do.

Here is our story – our life really is like an open book now! It is hard to read in parts but if it touches you in any way, please do something. Make a difference. Save a life. Believe in miracles.

Amanda, Kyle and Miracle x

CHAPTER 1

Fate, love, luck

Have you ever wondered whether miracles are real?

I can answer that question for you but I know that some people might take a bit of convincing. I do have a miracle in my life. In fact, I have two of them. Along with my husband Tobias and our son Kyle, we are really just an ordinary family. But somehow, we've been blessed. You might not believe that if you only know part of our story. You might think that we have been very unlucky indeed, but I've always been a 'glass half full' sort of person and when life throws something difficult at me I just put my fighting gear on and charge out of my corner. In fact, I'm often at my best when times get tough. Sometimes, clawing your way out reminds you what life's about and gets the blood pumping through your veins again.

Let me ask some other questions – do you create your own luck, make your own success or do you think that life is all down to Fate? Is it all mapped out for us; do we have our paths already plotted? I can't give an answer one way or another, but I am definitely coming round to the belief that Fate had plans for me. I'm not special though, I'm just an ordinary mumma – so, if for me, then why not for everyone else too? We just need to believe. And, these days, I do; I believe.

I have never been one for twee platitudes or meaningless comments. I think we all make choices in life and I think we have a responsibility to make sure those choices are good ones. Neither do I believe that any of us has the right to harm another soul. We're all part of this world, two-legged, four-legged, winged, feathered, furred . . . and we should all do our very best to ensure we leave the place better than we found it for every generation that comes after us . . . two-legged, four-legged, winged, feathered and furred too!

But something happened to me two years ago – or, rather, someone. A bundle of white fur, beaten and broken and bruised, a dog who had never been loved. An animal, who had only ever suffered at the hands of humans, padded his way into my life and into my heart. He wasn't the first – and he won't be the last – but little did I know that this one was going to turn my world upside down. There had been so many dogs and each one had left a hole in my heart, but this one was very special – this one had fought death to be with me and I was going to make sure no one let him down ever again.

It was the 4th April 2014 – 4.4.14 – which, strangely enough, is World Stray Animals Day. The day is set aside to raise awareness of the plight of millions of poor animals across the globe who never receive any care or compassion, and it was so fitting that this was the day on which my beautiful boy was to take his first steps on my homeland.

We had spent very little time together, only meeting the day before, when I went to collect him at the ferry port before beginning our journey up north to my home in Scotland, but I felt as if we had known each other forever. I knew from the moment I'd set eyes on him in a photograph a few months before that this dog was incredible. At that point, I didn't even know if he was a boy or girl. In fact, for a while, I didn't even know if he was alive or dead, destined for a fate I couldn't imagine. But there had always been something about him, something which said *save me . . .*

'Here we go then, Miracle,' I said to him, as we stepped off a train onto a busy platform at Edinburgh's Waverley Station. People were rushing to catch their connections for workday commutes, to visit friends and relatives, and they probably didn't give a second glance at the woman with her dog who had been travelling all night. We didn't look as if we were anything special – and, to be honest, at that point I didn't think we were. Our relationship was already one of love and trust, but I wasn't stupid – I knew I had a lot of work to do with this little guy and we probably had many difficult days ahead.

'Welcome to Scotland, Miracle – welcome home,' I whispered as I bent down to stroke the fur behind his ear. A camera flash went off nearby and I laughed nervously, worrying that Miracle would be nervous or even try to run away, but, true to the character I would see develop over the next few months, he didn't flinch. Looking up at me with what looked like absolute trust in his eyes, this dog sat at my feet and behaved as impeccably as the most well-trained, perfectly-bred hound in the world.

Our story was already getting a lot of attention, and it turned out that the flash was thanks to a photographer from the *Daily Mail* who was waiting as we arrived.

'Here we go, my darlin',' I said to Miracle. 'You're going to be a poster boy for all those poor dogs you've left behind.'

Miracle's past was horrendous and I know anyone that saw those photos would agree with me. He had been photographed on a Thai meat truck, close to death and heading for the most appalling fate imaginable. But a long road had brought him to me and I was never going to let him out of my sight again.

I'm just an ordinary Scottish mumma, but when it comes to animals, people say that I'm an Amazon. Ever since I could remember, I would help and rescue any animal in need; my first rescue memory was of a blue tit that I later released. By the time Miracle arrived at my home in the Scottish Highlands, the place was packed to the rafters with dogs! Not only did I have other rescues, but, along with Tobias, I ran a professional sled dog business that takes passengers on adrenalin rides of their lives! It had been our life-long dream as soon as we got sled dogs and we'd taken the big jump a few years before.

Our 6-year-old son Kyle was used to it all as he'd been listening to those pack howls all throughout my pregnancy and he'd been raised with dogs since the day he arrived home from hospital; despite my exhaustion, I was desperate to introduce this new one to him. As I walked in, Miracle on a leash at my side, I called to Kyle.

'Mumma's home!'

But there was no little boy running to greet me, no excited voice shouting my name, because Kyle is severely disabled. He has cerebral palsy and is autistic, which for him means he can't speak. He sleeps in a cot, uses specialist equipment to get around and he rarely makes eye contact with anyone.

He's my world.

And though I trust all of my dogs with my son, I'm not stupid. Miracle was being introduced into our home for the first time and that is always a sensitive moment. I didn't know the full extent of this dog's trauma, so, for the time being, I would be cautious. I had no reason to believe he would do anything bad to Kyle, but I had to protect both of them. We have special techniques when introducing Kyle to the dogs – he has a special chair that can be adjusted to various heights at the touch of a button and we always make sure Kyle is seated higher than the other dogs, for example.

When Kyle saw Miracle for the first time, he reacted in his own way, making sounds that Tobias and I can understand, but which mean very little to anyone else.

'Are you happy I'm home, sweetheart?' I asked.

I talk to him all the time, sing to him, try to engage him. None of us know the mysteries of a locked mind and I just hope that, one day, something will click. Even if it doesn't, I couldn't bear the thought that Kyle ever felt I was ignoring him, so I do keep up a steady stream of chatter. On this day, all of my talk was about our new doggy.

'Isn't he handsome?' I said. It wasn't strictly true – Miracle was in a terrible state, with an awful skin condition, but I could fix that. He had a lovely soul, of that I was sure. 'Look at how friendly he is!' I exclaimed, as Miracle had a good sniff around Kyle's buggy. 'You two will be the best of friends, I'm sure of it.'

I had no idea how prophetic my words would prove to be ...

Ever since this magnificent dog has come into our lives, I seem to be finding clues and links and messages everywhere. The pieces of our lives have fallen into place since Miracle has arrived, albeit with a slight nudge here and there. It's ironic that two years on from this very special dog's rescue, I'm sitting here putting pen to paper telling the world of his journey through life so far. This has also been a journey for my son, for me and for my husband.

For me, I like to think of this as therapy. So much has happened and some of it has been like a whirlwind that I've barely had time to catch my breath. At other times, the last thing I've wanted is time to think. I bet there are plenty of people reading this who know exactly what I mean. When life kicks you in the teeth, it's sometimes so hard and so unpredictable that you don't know whether the world is going at a million miles an hour or everything has slowed down to such an extent that each second takes a lifetime. I've slowed it all down again writing this. It's a strange process to look back at your own life and make a story out of it, but it has helped me a lot. More than anything, it has shown me just how fortunate we are to have a very special dog in our lives, and just how important a fighting spirit is.

Maybe that's what we recognise in each other – me, Kyle and Miracle . . . fighting against the odds, fighting for survival, fighting to love each other every single day.

CHAPTER 2

The obsession begins

My desire to save Miracle had been going on for many months, but he wasn't the first animal I'd set my heart on, not by a long chalk.

I was born into an ordinary family in Edinburgh in 1970. I had one sister who was four years younger than me and no dogs at all at that stage, which is hard to even imagine! Dad was a cooper who made barrels and later worked for the Post Office, so mum raised us both before going back to work when I was about twelve, getting a job as a care assistant to children with disabilities. I don't really have many memories of my childhood but I do remember that Mum always liked to make me pretty. She made sure I was immaculate, with ribbons in my hair and polished shoes on my feet. That was fine by me – I loved gorgeous things. I also loved to dance but I wasn't just a girly girl; there was nothing I enjoyed more than stealing bikes from local boys. However, my obsession, even at that age, was animals. Mum adored them too but felt it was unfair to have a dog as we lived in a tenement flat.

My Nana, though, had a dog that I walked and looked after, and there were a few hamsters along the way, but it wasn't what I truly wanted; I wanted a canine companion of my own, to love and cherish, to be my best friend. If there was anything on TV with animals, I'd be glued to the screen – *Black Beauty*, *Lassie*, *The Littlest Hobo*, *Gentle Ben*, *Skippy* ... I couldn't get enough of them. I'd spend my time bawling my eyes out at the sad scenes, desperately hoping that somehow there would be a happy ending and conveniently forgetting that there always was! Even when I watched something like *Cartoon Cavalcade*, it was the host's dog that I homed in on, ignoring everything else. I remember being taken to the circus once and getting very upset; I'd seen these animals in the wild on TV and it just didn't make sense to me. It all seemed so wrong.

There was a pet shop at the top of Leith Walk, near to where we lived, and I always tried to make family journeys pass by there – all sorts of animals were sold in shops back then, and, even though I knew I wouldn't be getting a dog any time soon, I whiled away the hours talking to the Minah bird that belonged to the owners.

Though Mum and Dad both loved animals, the fact that we lived in an Edinburgh tenement meant that having a dog would be unfair. So, other than my

Nana's dog, which I spent weekends with and loved to bits, I'd ask to walk other people's pets. A young couple who lived round the corner would have me knocking on the door as early as I could get out to play, just so that I could play with their Jack Russell. The poor souls had probably been out the night before and had to face me asking to take Trixie for a walk at the crack of dawn! Of course my mum had no idea I did this, but I loved my time with Trixie; she was a little livewire but so sweet.

On the weekends I'd be desperate to go and spend time at Nana's house. It was situated in a very green part of the city, with trees and a huge park, unlike the concrete jungle heart of the city where we lived. She'd get milk deliveries from a horse and cart, and I remember being in regular frenzies, running to get carrots so I could greet the horse and feed it when it came to the street. Over the years, Nana's dog, Beama (who I thought of as the family dog) taught me how to behave around animals, how to respect, how to love, and how to cope with loss. That wasn't something I dealt with well though – losing her as a child hit me hard. Beama had been rescued too and she was just the first in a long line in my life. My uncle was a long distance lorry driver and, on his way home one night, someone was giving puppies away in a pub. If nobody took this little black bundle by last orders, she was going to be thrown in the canal. So guess who came back home with him? She was so tiny, I'm told, that she slept in the grocery rack.

I suppose the rescue addiction started in those early years. I could see how an animal could have its life transformed by one act of kindness, and also how much it could bring to a family in turn. It's often been said that Mum and Dad are to blame for my huge collection of dogs as an adult – maybe if they'd allowed me to just have one as a kid, I wouldn't have as many as I do today! Perhaps that's true but I wouldn't have it any other way; I am surrounded by all I love and dogs have always made my heart beat that little bit faster.

By the time I was about to leave primary school, we had moved house, but there was still no dog in my life other than those I could walk whenever I got a chance. Heading to secondary school, by now I was quite frustrated. I had no idea what I wanted to do with my life and spent my time making myself look beautiful on the outside, wearing the latest fashion and make-up trends, but that soon got me down. People seemed to only care about the surface and believed if I looked fine, then I must be fine. As I got older I bunked off school a lot, hanging around shops, wasting time; I also gave up on dance as there was just too much pressure. The happy times I'd had as a child, flitting between pinching boys' bikes and going to ballet classes, had long gone.

I left school when I was sixteen. I had only really enjoyed athletics and art, so felt there was nothing left there for me. I was known as 'The Runner' and even trained with a coach at Meadowbank stadium in Edinburgh, but it still wasn't enough for me to want to stay. I knew what I wanted and that was to work with animals. When I was still at school, I went to the guidance teacher and he suggested I do a photography course.

'Why on earth would I do that?' I asked him.

'Well, it's the best option,' he replied, in a very offhand manner. 'Really Amanda, this notion you have of working with animals every day – it's just nonsense. That's not real life, that's not where your future lies at all.' I didn't believe him. I didn't want to believe him. I knew that, one day, I would be surrounded by them and it would be my life, my real life. 'Get that silly notion out of your head,' he snapped.

I'll show you, I thought to myself.

If there's one positive I got out of school, it was teaching me just how competitive I was. I had recognised it in myself from an early age, and, looking back on school reports, it is the one thing which is repeated and which stands out.

Amanda is highly competitive.

Amanda doesn't like to come second.

Amanda is very committed to ensuring she always comes first and is extremely disappointed in herself when she doesn't achieve this.

It would serve me well . . .

After I left high school, I had a run of jobs in shops, and offices. I was interested in make-up and special effects – I wanted to be the girl who made people look gruesome on TV! – but my family were worried about me living far away in London so I stayed put. I also did promotion work for agencies, anything from loo roll to alcohol, and even went for a job at an airline. But none of them seemed like a calling and they certainly didn't make me feel like I had won first prize; I knew this wouldn't be how I spent my life. Even at that stage, I felt that there was something bigger, something more important waiting for me. I had quite a few positions working for cosmetics houses such as Elizabeth Arden, Yvés Saint Laurent and Lancôme – yes, I was one of those make-up gorgons who terrorise you when you walk through a department store! It was the closest I could get to my goal of working in make up and special effects and I enjoyed it to a certain extent but my heart was never in it – these were just jobs, just ways of earning a crust. I also started modelling, thinking that I may as well make my looks work for me given that other people judged me on them anyway.

Looking back, I suppose I was just frustrated; I wanted my life to get more exciting. I had no idea that was much closer to happening than I could have imagined.

By now, I was 25 and had seen an appealing ad in a newspaper. After getting through the interview, I turned up to a city centre office and was given details of what the work would entail; it was basically selling voucher cards so that people could get deals on things like restaurant meals. To be honest, it was nothing special and I didn't have any desperate desire to do it for a living but I needed a change and it was something different. Little did I know what it would bring – or, more to the point, *who* it would bring!

Recovering from my bad break-up, animals became my fixation. They consumed my thoughts, and I really wasn't that interested in anything else – not even remembering to eat half of the time. I was being introduced to everyone in the office as time went on, but not absorbing many names, or even faces, then, one day, I met a good looking blonde guy with prominent cheekbones. He must have been one of the last people there for me to meet.

'Amanda, meet Tobias,' our boss said. 'Tobias, meet Amanda.'

'Hi,' I said, putting my hand out to shake his. (I've always had a firm handshake!)

He couldn't even say 'hello' back to me! His hand was shaking as the initial greetings were made and all I can remember thinking was 'got you!' I'd obviously made quite the impression, and, the more I looked at him, the more of an impression he made on me.

Each night, after work finished at 8pm, the whole team would go for a drink. Over the next few months, things between Tobias and I just developed. We'd spend most of the night talking to each other, we'd be the ones left when everyone else went home. I'd been so emotionally broken but I remember being so happy in his company from the start. We worked all day side by side, then socialised together, and I still couldn't get enough of him.

Tobias had been raised on the West Coast of Scotland. He'd had an idyllic childhood in the countryside, raised close to Eilean Donan Castle, where *Highlander* was filmed, but was now happy to live in the city, whereas I was the opposite. He proposed after four months and I immediately said 'yes'! I picked up a cheap cubic zirconia ring from a display in a chemist's window and said, 'This will do,' cuddling in to Tobias as close as could be. 'We can get a real one someday.' (And we did, don't worry!)

We were so happy, young and in love. The world seemed simple and we thought we could take on anything. I adored the fact that he loved dogs . . . though perhaps not quite with my fervour! I'd shared with him my dream of keeping huskies and having a sled dog team – I loved wolves but respected their wild roots – and he encouraged and shared that dream with me. Khandi really was just the beginning! *This was the sort of man I would be proud to spend my life with*, I thought.

However, what really excited me was what I did in my spare time. I had taken on a lot of voluntary work at the local Scottish Society for the Prevention of Cruelty to Animals Centre. I think that, when I turned up from work, in full beauty-counter mode with long dark hair and impeccable make-up, they must have thought I had no idea. Unsurprisingly, I was soon set to work doing the muckiest tasks but I was perfectly happy. Cleaning out kennels and shovelling dog poo didn't bother me in the slightest. As long as I was around animals, that was all that mattered. The dirty work had to be done, and I was more than willing to do it.

Doing voluntary work for an animal charity really grabbed hold of my heart and there was a little dog, a Jack Russell just like my old neighbour's dog, Trixie in the isolation block, where pending cruelty cases were kept. Her name was Sandy. She'd been beaten so badly that her hip was dislocated, she had cigarette burns across her body, only fourteen teeth left and bore a scar on her neck so deep that clearly should have been stitched but had been left to heal unattended. She was so terribly frail. Each night before I left, I'd fluff up her blanket and get her comfortable. Within the first month I knew I wanted to adopt her – she was so vulnerable. She was operated on but her hip had been kept dislocated for 6 months and had caused a lot of damage. After the op, her hip popped in and out of the socket all the time.

'Look at you, Sandy!' I'd laugh, giving her a cuddle. 'We never know where that hip is going to end up, do we? Never mind, I'll get you one day and you can spend all your days lying on a velvet cushion and doing whatever takes your fancy.'

I held onto that dream and had a notion that Sandy did too, but my application to adopt her could only be processed once her previous sick-minded owner had been dealt with legally. When that day came, her middle-aged life began with me. And with that new beginning came a new name: 'Khandi'.

It was a shaky start as she'd had such a hard life and clearly suffered many flashbacks over the early months but she really was the beginning of this whole story. And, over time, she blossomed into an amazing family member teaching lots of our other dogs' valuable lessons and boundary setting over the years. Despite all she'd been through, once she'd settled in with me Khandi was fantastic with people and always sought solace with kids in particular. I've a feeling her previous life involved living with gentle kids – it was the adults who were the problem.

I'd recently started helping out at a city farm too. It was in the middle of a very deprived area of Edinburgh, but was a welcome green space in the heart of it all and I soon found one of my best friends there. Cree was a Border Collie who was as bored on the farm as I was on the make-up counters. We hit it off straight away. Cree used to nip the heels of the sheep on the farm, clearly desperate to find something to do, to find a purpose. We had a lot in common. She would follow me round as I cleaned, best buddies from the moment she realised I would mix an egg into her kibble and always took time to play with her.

Cree also listened, walking next to me contentedly as I poured my heart out. It was clear Cree wasn't that happy with her surroundings (and not too keen on the farmer's wife, if I'm completely honest!) so we were like kindred spirits.

I'd chatter, as we walked around together. 'You're bored living in this place with nothing to do, aren't you? Something good needs to happen soon!'

It was here that Tobias finally realised just how much I really loved animals when he picked me up one day. As he walked towards me, I had a duck under one arm and a goose under the other.

'I've never seen you look so happy,' he told me. 'Look at that smile!' He followed me around as I did the nightly routine, and so did Cree, going from pen to pen. The Shetland ponies were giving me a hard time and the goats were stubborn as usual, but we had a great laugh.

I think that was the moment that Tobias really saw who I was. So many people still judged me on how I looked – the slender, tall girl with her make-up always perfect, long dark hair in place, well-dressed, perfumed and composed. They thought I was punching above my weight even attempting manual labour. But Tobias saw the real me. What I truly wanted was a life of animals, wellies on my feet, and this man I loved by my side.

'That's just what we'll have,' he told me, one night on the sofa, as we cuddled up in each other's arms. 'We'll have all of that – our own business, a huge house in the country, a sled dog team, and dozens of kids!'

'Dozens?' I repeated. 'I don't think so! I'm not even that maternal.'

'That's just not true,' he replied. 'You say that all the time, but you really are – you just use it all up on dogs and cats and other waifs and strays. Once we have our own kids, you'll see just how good at it you were meant to be. I know you'll be a great mum. We'll have it all, Amanda, we'll have it all.'

We married in 2004 in Caesar's Palace in Las Vegas, after an engagement of eight years! My dad had passed away the year before and then we lost Khandi a few weeks later, so we wanted to keep it as low-key as possible. People ask what we were waiting for, but there wasn't really anything. We were just happy together, settled in each other's company, and secure in our love – and, anyway, we had dogs galore! In fact, Tobias hadn't waited long after our engagement to put our big plans into action. We'd moved to Glasgow by now and Tobias had gone in to the restaurant business, managing a few premises there and also in Inverness. He was an absolute whizz at business and now he also had such a passion for sled dogs and sled dog racing – it really felt we were really making something happen. By now, we were already building up our collection of huskies: our first, Kuzak, joined us in 1998 and Kamatz and Odin had joined us by now, having been born in August and October 1998.

'Can you imagine?' he'd whisper to me, as we lay in bed at night. 'Can you imagine what our lives will be?'

'You've been saying this for years, Tobias!' I reminded him, 'and we're doing pretty well. You're on your way to getting that first business, we already have dogs, and I just know that we'll move to the Highlands one day.'

'I say it because it's true!' he laughed. 'We'll have children and dogs and a perfect home in the country and our own business. We'll be living the dream, Amanda – our dream.'

I had the dogs but I knew Tobias's desire for a child and I wanted to give that to him, if I could. It sounded perfect – but somehow the pregnancies never happened, the babies never came.

CHAPTER 3

Just a little bit longer

'It'll happen,' Tobias assured me. 'It's just taking a little longer than we expected.'

But it didn't happen, so we got some tests done. And that's when we were told, in 2006, it never would – not unless we had some help. Ironically, fertility treatment can break some couples. The consuming desire to have a child together, to cement your love, and to do anything to make it happen can be too much. The endless tests and the injections, the scans and the hopes and the fears and the disappointments can take over, and one day you realise that you've forgotten each other. We were lucky – it worked very quickly for us, but there were some problems. It will sound mad to anyone who isn't an animal lover, but I missed the dogs so much. Every time I had to leave them, I felt a pang of guilt. We were all so close and I wanted to spend every minute of every day with them, which meant that I actually felt selfish for devoting any time to our quest for a baby.

Tobias would try to talk sense into me.

'You'll be back before they know it,' he would say, 'and just think how happy they'll be to see you!' He would remind me of our dream. 'Children, a house in the country, our own business, and surrounded by dogs; it'll be perfect.'

I would say goodbye to each of them individually, tell them to be good and that I loved them, and then go off to the clinic for more tests, more treatment.

'You'll soon have a new puppy in the pack,' I would tell them, desperately trying to stay optimistic and remember the words Tobias would say to me. 'We'll have a perfect new home with lots of room for you to run around in, and a new little baby for you to look after.'

I swear they understood every single word I said to them. When I was going through my appointments, I would keep them all in my mind, dreaming of the day when we would have our rural idyll, dogs and children running about together.

It sounds so silly now, but I also had a terrible fear of needles and that was something which petrified me throughout the entire process.

'One of the best things you can do is to take some medication which will stimulate egg production,' one doctor told me.

'By "take" some medication, do you mean I'll just be having a few tablets?' I asked, already feeling nervous.

'Yes,' he said, and I breathed a sigh of relief. 'And we'll teach you how to inject yourself.' The fear kicked in again.

'I don't think I'll ever be able to do that,' I whispered. 'I am truly terrified of needles – is there any other way?'

He looked at me as if I was mad.

'Mrs Leask – how can I put this? By the time you have finished this process, you won't even be able to count how many needles have been stuck in you. It's very straightforward; every woman who goes through the process can manage it. I'm sure there are some who are a little worried, just like you, but it's a necessary evil. And not really a big deal.' It was a huge deal to me, and he wasn't doing anything to lessen it. 'When you do get to the stage of injecting, you can even choose where to do it, so you have complete control. You can choose your leg or your abdomen . . .'

'God, no!' I shouted. 'My abdomen? There is no way on Earth I could shove a syringe into my belly, so don't even think it!'

I did have to choose, and I chose my thighs. For weeks, I had to inject every day and it was awful. Tobias would have done it for me, but, by that point, he was in Inverness trying to rescue a business that was now struggling for all the time, money and energy we were putting in to trying to become pregnant, and I was still living in our house about thirty minutes outside of

Glasgow. I would complain to him every night on the phone, as the dogs all sat around me. To me, they were my sympathetic ears knowing that their Mumma was having a really hard time of it.

'You can do it,' Tobias would reassure me, 'I know you can. You're the bravest person I know, and this is for the most amazing thing. Remember the dream, Amanda, remember the dream.'

At this point, I really had to dig deep! Every time I even thought of injecting I was consumed with fear. I decided that, every time I stuck a needle in my thigh, I would picture Tobias, and I would picture the baby we longed for. I was told to choose a time to inject every day and stick to it. I went for 10pm – by then, I was trying to wind down. The kennels would be done, the dogs settled for the night. We'd been married over 4 years by now and we had seventeen dogs; it was a full-time commitment. I was so worried that they would feel neglected now that I had something else on my mind; even when I thought about trying for a baby when I was dealing with my canine family, I felt guilty.

The first time I had to inject was as terrifying as I'd thought it would be. I got on the phone to a nurse at the clinic and she talked me through it all; it made no difference and I was terribly bruised afterwards. To be honest, I bruise like a peach at the best of times, so that didn't come as much of a surprise, but it was a constant reminder of what 10pm would bring every evening. A friend of mine who was an insulin-dependent diabetic offered to come round and do the jabs for me as he was completely non-plussed about it all, but I was too scared so made my excuses and tried to just buckle down to it. To make matters worse, at some times I was on two different medications which meant I was stabbing myself twice a night.

Come on, Amanda, I said to myself, *you can do this – just focus on the prize.*

I just had to get into the zone. Despite my fear of needles, I wasn't at all squeamish with the dogs and had patched up a good few gruesome injuries in my time. I'd often had to give them intravenous or intramuscular injections in the past (and have done many, many more times since then), so I tried to remember their courage which helped me to finally get through it and move on to the next stage.

It wasn't an easy time, but, finally, Tobias and I were at the point where we were, hopefully, about to become parents-to-be. Once the injections were over and my eggs had been harvested, our medical team was at the point where we had to make a decision about embryos.

'It is something you need to think about very carefully,' we were told by the consultant. 'If we implant more than one, there is always the chance that you will end up with a multiple pregnancy. However, if we only implant one, there is a chance the pregnancy will not develop and you will have to go through the whole procedure again.'

For me, there was really no decision to be made. I couldn't face this again, so I asked that they place two back inside me. And right from the start of my pregnancy, I was convinced I was having twins. Sixth sense maybe, but, almost from the moment the pregnancy was confirmed, I had such a strong gut feeling that I was carrying two boys.

'You can't tell, not yet,' said Tobias, 'you'll just have to wait for a scan.'

But I could tell.

And when I was scanned two weeks later, I received the most wonderful news, even if I'd known it all along.

'I'm absolutely delighted to tell you that you are pregnant,' said the sonographer. Tobias and I grinned at each other like lunatics. 'But . . .' she went on, 'I think it might be triplets.'

Triplets?

My God, I thought; *three for the price of one.*

She left the room to get someone who could confirm the scan, and I really don't think Tobias and I said a word to each other; we were shell-shocked. When another sonographer looked, she said that all she could confirm was that we were definitely going to have twins. Twins ran in both our families and coupled with IVF, it almost seemed inevitable.

'Twins?' I repeated. 'That's still amazing – but what's happened?'

'It looks as if one has divided, and that, possibly another implanted but hasn't developed,' she told us. 'Congratulations! You are definitely pregnant with twins!'

I had been absolutely right to have two implanted then, as there was a huge chance that, if I had only gone for one, it wouldn't have worked. As it was, it had all gone perfectly first time – and I'd never have to have those bloody injections again!

'This is it,' said Tobias, as we gazed at the screen. 'This is the start of our family.'

'Hey!' I scolded him. 'We already have a family – we have a whole pack of dogs at home, don't forget them!'

The idea that we were going to bring two babies into the mix in nine months' time was wonderful. We spent hours talking about it.

'We'll get those baby carriers that you strap to your chest,' said Tobias, wistfully. 'You'll have one, I'll have the other, and we can walk for hours and hours. You, me, the babies and the dogs.'

It was a delightful thing to think of and look forward to, but I knew it would be hard. I started reading up on twin pregnancies and was staggered at how much weight I'd put on.

'What if I don't see my ankles for months?' I cried to Tobias. 'There's no way I'm going to let that happen. I'll keep fit. With all these dogs, I don't have the option of lying around.'

It was certainly a challenge. Tobias was still in Inverness, living in a flat over one of the bars he managed and I was still almost a three-hour drive away from him. He got back when he could, but, to be honest, at that point, we expected a straightforward pregnancy. I was maybe a bit older than most first-time mums as I was in my late thirties by now, but I was fit. There was no reason to think that this would be anything other than textbook.

In fact, we were so convinced and on cloud nine that we'd even started the next part of our dream – we'd bought a new house, about half an hour outside of Inverness, one that needed a lot of work . . . well, not just a lot of work, it didn't even have floors and Tobias spent months renovating it! And that was just to get it in a state we could live in; it would take years to make it perfect. It drove me mad not being able to nest and I threw many hissy fits, particularly about the nursery which was so precious to me – and knowing I had to double everything now too. My god, *Darling Buds of May* it wasn't! But it could and would give us everything we hoped for, with land for all the dogs. It was a completely mad time but we wanted to be in there before the birth and have our first memories with our kids there. (When I finally moved in, an osprey flew overhead, reminding me how lucky we were to be able to start our dream life.)

I had no idea, at that point, no idea at all what was hurtling towards us. The pregnancy was difficult from the start. I didn't have morning sickness but sometimes wished I had. I don't know what's worse – being sick and getting it over with, or feeling nauseous all the time but never getting any relief from it. If there was food around, it was even worse. I only had to catch a whiff of something and I felt as if I was going to vomit. I had to shut myself in another room and open all the windows, but – I tried to tell myself – this was a good sign. All of the pregnancy books said that morning sickness (or all-day-nausea in my case) meant that everything was progressing well.

I would still walk the dogs and do chores to a degree, but training with the sled dogs with them racing around me was now impossible (and a bad idea!) so we had people come and help out.

I always did my best to think positively but, over the next few weeks, it was difficult to do. I just didn't feel great at all. I read every book, every article, every website, but none of them suggested I should be feeling as bad as I did. I also seemed to be getting really big, really quickly. I put it all down to having twins, but there was a niggle at the back of my mind, something telling me that this wasn't how it should be.

'There's something wrong,' I would confide in Tobias. 'I just know it – something isn't right.'

Other people would tell me that it was just nerves at being a first-time mum, that I was just reading too much into it all . . . but I knew. I truly did. At sixteen weeks, I was scheduled in for a scan, and I was desperate for it. I just wanted to be sure that my babies were alright. I got a call a few days before it was due to take place which worried me even more – the sonographers were on holiday so it would all have to be later than I expected. I'd been holding onto that date, focussing all of my energy (and there wasn't much of it) on getting there and putting my mind at rest, and now I was having to wait even longer.

'I can't bear this,' I told Tobias. 'Something isn't right and I just want them to confirm it so that I can get help.'

I really was worried so I visited my GP just to be on the safe side and was assured that my blood pressure and all else was fine.

'Really, Mrs Leask,' the GP said, 'every new mother has concerns, but there is nothing to suggest that this isn't all going according to plan. Twin pregnancies do get hard going – they are trickier and they are much harder work, but your blood pressure is fine.'

It wasn't my blood pressure I was worried about. I read everything I could about twins on the Internet and one thing stuck in my mind: twin to twin transfusion syndrome or TTTS. It's a disease of the placenta which affects identical twin pregnancies. With it, identical twins who share a common monochorionic placenta have to deal with abnormal blood vessels which connect the umbilical cords and circulations. The placenta sometimes gets shared unevenly, along with everything else, which leaves one twin having too much while the other has too little. Blood between the vessels gets shared in a completely disproportionate way and gets transfused from one to the other; the twin giving the blood (the donor) has too little, the other twin (the recipient) has too much. The decreased blood volume in the donor twin results in slower growth for that baby, and far too little amniotic fluid.

I knew a detailed scan would help allay my fears and heard of a private clinic where you could get scans for this, so I gave them a ring. It wasn't too far away and I got an appointment quite quickly. I just wanted reassurance – I wasn't sure how I should be feeling, maybe this was normal. Nonetheless, I wanted it checked out.

And I was so glad I did.

As soon as the scan began, it was clear to see that one baby was smaller than the other. I was immediately worried. I thought of what I'd read about twin to twin transfusion and I thought this was it.

'Are they OK?' I asked, but the sonographer said nothing. Tobias squeezed my hand and I know my eyes were full of tears. *Please let them be OK*, I told myself.

'Look,' I said to him, 'we're having boys!'

It was so easy to tell, even then, but we couldn't really get any pleasure out of being able to add a bit more detail to our babies' identities as there was a strange atmosphere in the room.

'There's something wrong, isn't there?' I said to the sonographer, silent beside me.

'I really just need to get on with the scan, Mrs Leask,' she told me. 'You'll get some images at the end that you can take back to your doctor.' There was no doctor at the clinic – I knew there wouldn't be any treatment – but I couldn't let it go; I needed to know what she could see.

'One of them is bigger than the other, Tobias,' I told him, even though he was looking at the same screen and must have noticed too. 'Do you think that's OK? Do you think one of them is just a bit chunkier?' Who was I kidding? This wasn't a slight difference – this would have been obvious to anyone. I could see the sonographer looking a bit uneasy and I pushed her again to convey her thoughts but she wouldn't be drawn.

When the scan ended, I suddenly wished I hadn't asked at all.

'I'm really sorry Amanda,' she said, 'but I'm a bit concerned. I think you should go home and get your pregnancy records then go to your local hospital immediately. Something's not right. Something's not right at all.'

We did just that the very same day.

CHAPTER 4

A mother knows

I was in tears as Tobias drove to the hospital; nothing he could say would reassure me.

'He was so small,' I wept, referring to our tiny baby we had seen on the screen. 'What if we lose them, Tobias? What if we lose our babies?'

'*Sssh*,' he said, consolingly. 'Let's wait until we speak to the experts, let's not jump to conclusions.' But there was nothing he could have said that would have made me feel better. Surely twins grow at roughly the same rate? It couldn't be right that one of them would grow normally and the other would just lag behind until it decided to catch up one day?

The drive felt like hours but we finally arrived at the hospital and went to the scanning department. The receptionist looked like she couldn't have cared less, even though my face must have been streaked with tears.

'Oh no, you won't get a scan today,' she told me. 'There's no one available to do that. Call us on Monday, you might be in luck.'

Luck? I wasn't really wanting to place any of my hope on that. But there was no one to see us, no one to allay our fears. It was an awful weekend, waiting and worrying myself sick about what could be wrong. It seems awful, looking back now, that we couldn't get an emergency scan on the day but it just wasn't available. The days dragged so slowly and I just spent as much time as I could with the dogs. My appointment actually ended up being for the Tuesday and it couldn't come quickly enough.

But with that scan, my worst fears were confirmed. Everything I'd read up on changed into my reality.

The boys had twin to twin transfusion.

The doctors confirmed that equal blood flow wasn't going to both babies. One of my babies was surrounded by too much amniotic fluid, the other was surviving in very little – and without intervention both would die. It was just all so much to take in. We were told that I might have to go to London for an operation.

'That's insane,' I laughed, in that panicked way you do when everything just seems completely surreal. 'How can I have an operation while I'm pregnant? And I can't go all the way down there!'

I couldn't handle any of it – it was just too much. I couldn't comprehend what they were saying. They had us waiting for hours while they called around trying to get me a bed in a hospital that specialised in foetal medicine, the fear building inside me with every passing second. Finally, I was told that they'd found me a place to go in Glasgow which was at least better than London.

So, then they started, the frequent trips back and forth to Glasgow which ended up becoming my home again for quite a while. I didn't need an operation just then after all but over a very short period of time I started experiencing a lot of pain. I hadn't been experiencing pain because of the treatment they'd given me, but it also meant I couldn't eat anything acidic. I forgot one day and bit into an apple – I really paid the price as I thought I was going to die from the agonising pain that flooded over me. I was rushed to the local hospital and, because my stomach was expanding at one hell of a pace, they grabbed a wheelchair thinking I was in labour. They admitted me to a ward, pumping me full of painkillers but not knowing what they were actually treating. But if they let the meds subside, or didn't keep me topped up I was in terrible pain to the point they had me on gas or air. It is great stuff and it did work – I was off the planet at one point – but it didn't last. By the next day, I was still in agony and they seemed no closer to working out what was wrong so decided that I should be transferred to another hospital, this time in Edinburgh. Off I went by ambulance, sporting my beige satin PJs and wondering just what would happen – would we all get out of this alive? I would fight like hell for my boys; I could only hope they had the same spirit as we were clearly in for a rocky ride.

I was put on a drip, which contained painkilling medication as well as fluid. I desperately hoped it would kick in soon, as the pain was overwhelming at times. The doctors still weren't too sure what was happening – they thought that I might have had an ulcer or perhaps gallstones, so I had day after day of scans and ultrasounds and MRIs, all of which were horrible. As I lay in the MRI machine, I did start to panic. It was terribly claustrophobic in there and my stomach was already so huge that it was nearly touching the ceiling of the machine. I wasn't surprised by the results – no ulcer, no gallstones. Perhaps there was something really small that wasn't showing up yet, one doctor suggested?

'We're at a loss, Amanda,' I was told after all the tests that could be done, had been done. 'You need to go to a different hospital and, hopefully, they'll be able to figure out what's going on.'

I was sent back to Glasgow for even more investigations but I knew what it was; I knew it was my babies. I had been so unwell since the start, and there was a little voice telling me that something was very wrong. What could I say? How could I say to all of these experts, 'your tests are looking at the wrong thing – my gut knows more than all of you put together'? So, I kept quiet and went to Glasgow. More tests, more scans to check if now was the time they might have to intervene. It was a long way from the magazines and media images of the joy of having a baby. I wasn't one of those glowing mums-to-be, skipping along with a tummy the size of a neat football, and glowing with health. I looked awful – like I was carrying an elephant – and I felt worse.

But my return to my husband and the dogs was short-lived. I woke up one morning and was doubled up in pain as soon as I got out of bed.

'Oh God, what's happening?' I cried to Tobias. 'I just want the babies to be OK; I just want to feel well again.'

'We need to get you back to hospital,' he told me, calmly. 'They will work it out – eventually.'

So, back we went. This time, I didn't hide anything. I was completely open about how bad things were and they could see from my ashen face that I really couldn't cope for much longer. While waiting for yet another scan, I had a painful turn in the waiting room and one of the nurses let slip how worried everyone was.

'I don't think you'll be getting back home this time,' she told me.

To be honest, it was what I had been waiting for. I couldn't go on like this, and I was terrified that something might happen and I would be too far from hospital for them to do anything about it. I was on so many drugs by now, I was rattling! It would be a long, exhausting – and very dull – road, but I would do anything to ensure this all worked out, even if it meant me lying in bed for months with my legs up in the air, doped up on painkillers!

I was scanned every day and visited by every specialist they could drum up. I couldn't tell you how many times, I've lost count. More than anything, it was the pain that was getting to me. I'd always thought I had quite a high threshold but this was unlike anything I'd ever experienced. If I needed the drugs before the ward round, I was in agony while I waited; if there was no choice but to wait, I would be doubled up on the floor, the pain hitting me in a flash. To make things worse, although I was in a private room, I was still on a maternity ward. All around me were the sounds of women in labour every minute of the day. I wondered if I would ever get to that stage, and I also felt guilty complaining about my pain when they were going through such agonies. I would see some women come in, give birth, and be out in the same day – I had months ahead of me to try and keep my twins alive.

I settled into days of routine – every day I lathered my stomach in oils, determined to have control over my stretch marks at least. And if there is one ounce of luck that I got, it's that I never got one! Even the specialist, who would visit with his students, would comment on it! But I really was massive by now and looked like I could pop.

By this point, we decided to name the boys – they were little people, the centre of our world, and we couldn't keep calling them 'the twins'.

'Kyle and Ty,' I said to Tobias, referring to the names we had chosen at the start, the names we felt fitted impeccably with our boys.

'Perfect,' he said, kissing me – but we both knew it was all far from perfect. Ty was the little one and he was in a bad way. I was warned that when his bladder started to shrink, it would be time for surgery. He was clinging to life in just 1cm of amniotic fluid, the sensation for him would be as if he was wrapped or encased in cling film. I couldn't let myself dwell on it. I had to be strong and positive, even when all I could see around me were worried faces.

One late night on the ward rounds, the nurse wasn't happy with the babies' heartbeats. I was sent for a scan but it didn't really show any great detail so I had no choice but to wait until morning for my specialist. I remember her not being happy that she hadn't been called the night before.

'Amanda,' she said, 'I think it's time.'

Ty's bladder was shrinking and I had to prepare for a flight to London to meet with the professor who really was our last hope at keeping us Three Musketeers on target. I was 23 weeks along now and the flight down was so painful. I couldn't get in a comfortable position at all and the seatbelt was driving me nuts. I just wanted to lay flat on the floor. I was so dependent on medication by this point in my pregnancy; I must have resembled a junkie! Nothing else would help though – I was stuck in a cycle of needing the drugs desperately but also fearing what effect my dependency could have on the boys; I was a wreck. When we finally reached the hospital and had the consultation, I was so relieved. I knew this man understood why I was in pain.

He scanned me and then said, 'you don't have an ulcer or gallstones or anything anyone else has suspected. It's that you have this ridiculous amount of amniotic fluid building up and I need to reduce it.'

'Can you do that?' I asked.

'Of course.'

'Safely.'

'Of course.'

I was so relieved that someone finally understood, I remember bursting into tears. I just wanted the babies safe and for an expert to tell me it was all going to be OK.

I had 24 hours until it was time for theatre and what a performance that was going to be: I'd be awake through the whole thing. The professor would have to go into the womb via my tummy, and insert a camera and laser. Then he would have to cauterise the placental blood vessels so that equal blood flow would go to both babies, giving them an equal chance at life. Now, I can be pretty vain but I know that, when it comes to hospitals, you have to leave your dignity at the door and just get on with it. I decided it wouldn't matter what they asked me, I'd do it.

I was surprised that the spinal tap, which left me awake throughout the whole thing, actually also left me unable to feel anything. I bloody well felt that needle though, trying to find its way and, at first, it wasn't where it should be. The professor wouldn't start until I felt nothing but eventually we got there. It sounds crazy now but during the op, Kyle was grabbing the camera too, making the surgeon's job even harder.

This wonderful man managed to safely remove 4 and a half litres of amniotic fluid, measured out in jugs, filling everyone's shoes in the process. He took Tobias aside and told him he strongly suspected that my days of being reliant on pain relief were over.

I'd been a rattling drug cocktail up to now. Nothing had really helped; it just eased the pain and gave me bad night sweats with little sleep. But after the procedure to remove the excess fluid, I needed nothing stronger than oral paracetamol. The drug cocktails were a thing of the past as were the iron injections and iron transfusions I'd suffered. We were ecstatic! My problem was simply all of the excess fluid I was carrying.

With the operation over, I kept on telling myself that I would overcome the hiccups of this damn pregnancy and see the faces of my babies – alive and well . . . It finally felt like we had a chance between the three of us to really go for it. Not once did I think about me, just them; I never ever thought about how my life was in jeopardy.

As I lay in recovery, a woman was placed next to me, with her newborn baby being checked over as I lay waiting to find out if my boys even had heartbeats. I knew they shared a placenta so if one of them died, the other would have no chance of survival. The consultant got rid of her pretty sharpish and apologised for whoever had been so insensitive as to place her there. I didn't care once I got the wonderful news that there were heartbeats. There were!

Thankfully, the next day we were allowed to fly back home. It felt amazing to be free of the drugs that I'd worried would harm the babies. As the hours passed, I couldn't help be paranoid that I would need pain medication again but I didn't – the doctor was right all along. All I could think of now was holding a boy in each arm and them being future sled dog enthusiasts over the years to come. Every parent dreams and my dreams were right back on track.

The dogs had been my life for so long and we'd always hoped that our sons would be a big part of that too. I'm not afraid to admit that, for someone like me, it's hard being a bit of a control freak not in control. But I just had to let this one ride. This was something I couldn't control. The scar I bore now after surgery grew all the more precious to me. It is the scar that represented my fighting sons.

So, we were home. Feeling my sons using me as a springboard felt good, even if my stomach did resemble a scene from *Alien*. I would watch my stomach stretch in two different directions and it was one of the freakiest things I'd ever seen. Because of the nature of this pregnancy and because things were moving so fast, photos were not a priority. There was an odd one taken on a phone here and there but not much at all, so what I do have is so special. However, at the time, what mattered was that the awful days were behind us. The boys were fine, I'd heard their heartbeats, and all I had to do now was wait.

CHAPTER 5

Life

Sadly, our happiness was short-lived. It wasn't long before I was admitted back into hospital where this time I was going to have to stay until the babies were born. The amniotic fluid had built up again and I'd had another episode during a scan, so they didn't want to take any more chances. My goal was to reach 32–33 weeks to give Ty a fighting chance at life. Anything less would be grim to say the least. So I was back to my routine of trying to stop the boredom, not go mad in my own little room locked away from the other women giving birth and going home while I just had to hope I could keep my babies safe inside me for as long as I could.

The best scenario would be them growing safe until 2 March 2009, their due date. But I started to feel uncomfortable again just 12 days after the fluid removal procedure, sore and huge. I knew myself before they confirmed it, but the laser surgery hadn't been successful. It had, however, bought me 12 days. And in those 12 days, I had hope. It was the build up to Christmas and it's a season I love. I used to decorate the Christmas tree at Tobias's restaurant so, to keep me busy, the nurses had me decorate the tree on the ward. I made it as pretty as I could, thinking back to previous happy Christmases and trees.

By now, I knew I couldn't have laser surgery for a second time so what was the plan of action this time round? In a nutshell, stick in a very large needle and drain 4 and a half litres out again. Oh my god – needles! There was no local anaesthetic this time – this alone had me in a state. I still remember the procedure too, going very warm then the pain getting gradually worse. When I mentioned it, both doctors threw one another a look and stopped the procedure straight away. They encouraged me to stand up off the bed, but I couldn't. The pain was terrible – what the hell had they done? *This was ridiculous*, I thought; I had walked in there, I could surely walk back out, I didn't need a wheelchair. But I did. I really did. *Had they hit a nerve*, I wondered? Something was certainly wrong, that was for sure. I felt so stupid being wheeled two hundred metres back to bed but I really couldn't walk. These pains were getting worse and I had a sick feeling that I knew what was happening. I just hoped I was wrong.

One of the nurses I'd come to know very well was monitoring me. But the pain was getting steadily worse and I just couldn't keep a lid on things anymore, I got pretty vocal. Tobias kept on telling me to try and quieten things down – I was upsetting the other patients! I didn't bloody care. I knew what was happening now and it wasn't good.

Tobias hadn't realised what was going on until the nurse explained I was having tightenings.

'What does that mean?' he asked.

'Contractions,' she told him, and the word reverberated around the room. 'Amanda's threatening to miscarry.'

Hearing that confirmed my worst fears.

I was losing the boys.

By this point, I was feeling awful. I had no power over this, no control over my own body – everything we'd hoped for, fought for, was slipping through our fingers. I was immediately put on medication to attempt to bring the contractions to a standstill. I couldn't bear the thought of the boys making an appearance this early. It would be a disaster.

Thankfully, the medication worked and by later that night, all had settled down and things were looking promising. It was such a relief. I was told to stay as calm as I could, and not stress. What the hell did they mean? How was I meant to do that? My mind goes at 100mph at the best of times so this was impossible.

But I had to try.

I couldn't speak to anyone, I didn't want to. It was too hard to listen to anyone say anything nice to me that could reduce me to tears and take me to a place I just couldn't afford to go.

At that time, I was trying to write Christmas cards, I had a list of presents for Tobias to buy, amongst the list as long as his leg of all else to take care of including the business and our new home in the countryside getting completely renovated, as well as seventeen hyper, extremely active working dogs. All I could think of, to keep me sane, were the dogs, one called Odin in particular. I knew he'd be the one to struggle without me, thinking I'd abandoned him. This boy had got me through so much in the past and it broke my heart thinking of him, my little canine mate. Even the nurses spoke of ways we could smuggle him in for a visit, but we never did. I missed him like hell.

A week went by and yet again I was faced with going through the same procedure that had nearly caused me to lose the boys. *Oh God, not again*, I thought. I couldn't handle this a second time but I was left with no choice. If I stayed the way I was, the fluid would keep on building and risk everything anyway. So, still the best way forward was to do this, removing 2 and a half litres this time. At least I had a local anaesthetic – and I had to be thankful for small mercies. Just like the last time, that hot wave of pain surged around me once more and this time nobody had to confirm what was happening. Another contraction had hit with force again. This time they had a wheelchair on standby and the drugs waiting for me. And so it was a waiting game for the second time; would the contractions increase or would we keep them at bay? We managed to slow things down again – which was just as well, as my stress levels were going through the roof fighting such a battle. I was so scared for how many times I'd need this procedure because we were playing with fire. I knew I was running out of chances now. More than ever, I was counting the days not the weeks. As each day went by, I was buying more time – each day was another that the boys had survived.

Until 16 December 2008.

I actually felt pretty good that morning and had a scan booked in so I'd just wandered out of the ward and across the corridor in my PJs. The day didn't feel any different and neither did I. I'd built up a really good rapport with my consultant and, as she scanned me as she'd done many times before, I read what she was thinking before she'd even opened her mouth.

'This is it, isn't it?' I asked. 'There's no more time, is there?'

As always, she wouldn't say anything. They never do when it's bad, I've learned that. Her superior was called in at that point and I knew it wouldn't be long before I got an answer, one way or the other.

'I'm really sorry, Amanda,' said the consultant, holding my hand as she looked at the screen, 'but we're at a critical point. Ty's heart is beginning to fail. We can't wait any longer, it would just be too dangerous. We have to get the boys out now.'

I was terrified. But as in many scary situations before now, I could feel myself switching to autopilot to protect my sons. I was a mother and had a job to do. I called Tobias straight away and told him the frightening news.

'They're going to be born this afternoon,' I cried, feeling utter desperation that he was three hours away from us. I knew he'd put his foot to the floor, but I was so afraid to be on my own. All I could think was that I was about to lose a son for sure, possibly both. 'I need to have an emergency C-section, Tobias, it's all happening so soon.'

It was all even harder to deal with because I'd never told Tobias I had to get to 33 weeks at least to give Ty a chance. Maybe he knew, perhaps the doctors told him, but it wasn't something I could speak about. I just had to focus on those weeks going by.

I knew I had heartache ahead and it was killing me knowing before I went to theatre that my son wasn't going to make it. His growth had fallen 6 weeks behind Kyle's at this point. I was 29 weeks pregnant but Ty wasn't. Singletons can survive at such an early date of birth but when twins are so premature, it is even more problematic. To break the news to Tobias that I was being taken to theatre to have an emergency C-section was really hard. I just kept telling myself to hope that two miracles would happen.

Just as I expected, Tobias got to the hospital in record time and we sat there, both of us in shock, wondering how we would get through this. Looking around that room that had become home, with my own microwave, fridge and M&S meals, and a little TV that we had to buy an aerial for to get it working . . . it all just seemed so insignificant. I tried to do normal things like watch the TV or read a book to give me sanity, but there was a continuous foot flow of nurses, cleaners and doctors so it was impossible to focus. My concentration span resembled that of a flea! I'd loathed the hospital food too – most women only have to endure a few days whereas I'd had weeks of the stuff – and now I wondered just how I had survived such a small cell when my boys were fighting to breathe every second of every day that passed.

But time passed again, as it always does and, before long, I was taken for my operation. Lying in theatre was scary. I was really nervous, especially about the number of people in the room – 15, not including me and Tobias. So many faces I'd never seen before. That had me on edge and the prospect of a needle being stuck in my spine again was awful, given that the first experience for the laser op wasn't the best. Thankfully, this guy was fabulous and I wasn't aware he'd even done it. Something had, at last, gone smoothly.

I had a great relationship with my consultant but she still wouldn't let me watch my twins being born via the emergency hatch, as I called it. The screen was raised so that I couldn't see all the blood and guts and gore. After everything I'd been through, I wasn't squeamish anymore and really wanted to see them – I'm used to patching up injuries in dogs after all and I wanted to make sure she gave me the tiniest possible incision; I just wanted to be nosy and I just wanted a tiny scar. What's a bit of vanity here and there? I'd been pretty much stripped of everything else!

There were around fifteen staff members in that theatre, and my consultant and I shared the same macabre sense of humour. The mood was sombre and I couldn't bear that so we exchanged fun stories, trying to lighten the mood, and she told me that she was just as vain when she went into labour, 6 weeks early. She'd been caught off guard and had to make an emergency trip for a bikini wax – I had such admiration for a girl who still has time to be vain when she is in pain; that takes balls, so to speak.

Then she went a bit too quiet. The laughter stopped.

I saw her and Tobias throw that familiar look I'd seen before. The one that spells out loud and clear you're in deep trouble. My thoughts had only been of the boys, keeping their hearts beating. I don't think as a mummy you think of anything else, but now, it didn't look so good.

I wasn't aware of the moment the boys were actually delivered as they went straight into the hands of the doctors and nurses waiting on them. All I was aware of was a whispering and moving around me.

Kyle and Ty were here.

My boys had been born.

I wasn't allowed to see or touch them. I just wanted one touch, one kiss, because it might have been the only time I'd see them alive. But they were whisked away past me. I forgot about the fact that I was still lying there being stitched up. There was that look again. *OK, I thought, what was wrong this time?*

'Amanda, you're giving me a bit of a problem here,' she said.

'Why?'

'I'm having trouble stopping you bleeding.'

At that point I remember thinking, *at least the boys are out*. Maybe my miracles would defeat the odds stacked against them and fight – and make it even if I didn't. I remember thinking this at the time, desperate for the past few weeks of pain and suffering to have led them somewhere, to have made them safe. Someone must have been looking down on us though because soon the obstetrician did stop the bleeding and when she told me I was fine, all I wanted was to see my sons. I hadn't banked on being in so much pain though; I thought there would be meds to keep all of that at bay but even morphine wasn't magic!

It took a few hours before I was taken up to intensive care to see them. It was really upsetting to not be able to hold my babies in my arms; I could only look. Kyle was in one ventilator and Ty in another that shook like crazy and was so noisy. It was called the oscillator and for babies of the highest dependency. I really struggled with that, we both did.

Quickly, we found ourselves trying to divide time between the two ventilators that were around 4ft apart. At that point, Kyle stood a 97% chance of survival. Ty was a huge worry but was surprising the team by doing better than predicted. He just looked so bruised and wounded. They were both so helpless and it was hard not to be able to do anything. I couldn't believe they were actually here, but 11 weeks early was terrifying.

Of course, family and friends wanted to visit but this was a very peaceful and quiet ward so foot flow was kept to a minimum. I remember a family member telling me I would need to warn people how upsetting the place was – well, we were on the frontline and felt like we'd just been hit by a train, I'm sorry but I wasn't best placed to be thinking about other people's feelings. I had Kyle and Ty on my mind, nobody else.

That first night was a tough one. I was on morphine and other pain meds but had missed the late ward rounds to be given more because I'd been with the twins. I managed to fall asleep but woke during the night in a sweat and in agony again. It turned out that the nurse on that round had marked me down as having had pain relief when I hadn't.

'I can't get through this without drugs,' I pleaded with Tobias, as he pressed the buzzer for help. I was trembling with pain by then and the nurse had to undress and redress me when she finally came over to give me the right dosage.

The battle of our lives lay ahead.

'I'm going to start a diary, the nurses suggested it to me, and I'm going to write it in Kyle's voice' I told him. 'I don't want to forget any of this.'

One of the nurses helped me with my first entry:

Today, my brother and I decided that it was time to meet our Mum and Dad. I put my bottom up and out I went. There were lots of people to help us because we are small and really should have waited longer. I have lots of dark hair. I heard the nurses say that the doctors have put a tube into my airway to help me breathe – there is a machine that will do lots of the work for me so that I don't get too tired. My brother Ty was born two minutes after me but he isn't as strong. The doctors and nurses have to give him lots of help. I like my name, Kyle. I like that I am side by side with my brother, just like when we were in mummy's tummy.

How could I ever have thought I would forget any of it? It's etched in my mind to this very day and will be forever, but all I could think that night, as I wrote, was that my boys were here and I needed to make the most of it, no matter what.

CHAPTER 6

Kyle & Ty

The next day proved to be one of the toughest of our lives and there was no way we could have prepared for it, not really. We had known the odds were stacked against Ty from the start, but it was still difficult to hear.

'It's a terrible thing for you both, I know' said the consultant, 'but Ty just isn't going to make it, I'm afraid. The odds are stacked so heavily against him that there is no way he can survive. I'm so sorry, but the kindest thing you can do for him is let him go.'

This was the moment we'd been dreading. To hear those words knocked hell out of us. I'd hoped that since he'd made it to the outside world alive that a little miracle might just happen, but it wasn't to be. Tobias refused to give in but I knew . . . This was the one last selfless thing we could do for Ty, to end his suffering. It was the hardest decision we've ever had to make.

We had some incredible nurses helping us and, knowing we were too consumed with grief to do it myself, they wrote in my diary that afternoon, in Kyle's voice:

I had medicine to help me breathe more easily, and I am stretching my little arms and legs. My brother is not doing so well – he needs lots of drugs and help, and he looks very tired. By the afternoon, he was even more tired and very sick. The doctors and nurses won't be able to help him anymore. I will have to say goodbye to Ty soon. It will be strange not to have him there, but I know we will always be together. Mummy and Daddy are very sad having to say goodbye to him.

Ty spent time in his Daddy's arms then slept away in mine with Kyle lying next to him. I had to let go of my little miracle that had battled so much to reach our arms only to leave us again. That moment changed us both and I can't say it was always for the better. The events that followed that night I hold very close and will never forget. It's taught me a lot about dealing with loss, particularly with the dogs around us, and to never be selfish.

I could hardly believe he had gone. He had spent all of those weeks inside of me as the three of us fought, and now he was gone in a flash. All I had were my memories and my scars, scars that I would wear proudly for the rest of my life.

We went stumbling and mumbling into the next day not knowing how we'd handle it; seeing Kyle without his brother close by was really tough. They'd shared a womb, shared a blood supply for 29 weeks and now they were apart. I hated it. So, when I called the intensive care unit to arrange our visit with Kyle, as we were advised to do that morning, nothing could have prepared me for what lay ahead, nothing. I recognised the accent of who answered the phone and was given the option of someone coming to speak with us.

Why?

Why did someone have to do that? Fear flowed through my veins.

What the hell had happened? Kyle was settled the night before and had been given a pretty good prognosis, so what now? I was informed he now had 'significant problems'. I threw the phone down and Tobias got the wheelchair I had to use. At this point, I couldn't walk the length of myself but I couldn't get there quickly enough, through corridors and lifts. We buzzed to get in and could see two consultants waiting, ready to meet us. I just couldn't believe the door we were led through – it was the room we bathed Ty in before saying goodbye. It was gutting. The consultants must have sensed my horror because they blurted out, 'Don't worry, he's still alive'. I actually can't remember the abuse I hurled at them; I couldn't believe their insensitivity and demanded to know what the hell had happened to our son overnight.

In actual fact, I felt that the conversation they were having with us was designed to keep us at bay. On the ward, a sea of nurses and doctors were trying to stabilise Kyle after he'd haemorrhaged into his lungs. It had been decided on the ward rounds that morning they'd try him on a lesser ventilator since he'd been doing alright – without any consultation with us, of what we might like or want, they had made this momentous decision alone and he nearly lost his life. We nearly lost our other son, our only son. They had some explaining to do. Why had we not been told about this? Surely this should have been discussed with us before being carried out? Surely this couldn't be standard practice? I just wanted them to shut up with trying to justify themselves and answer the thousand questions we had. Nothing they could say now made an ounce of sense to me; why had they done this without our involvement?

I felt so protective towards Kyle; Tobias was right all along, I had a fiercely maternal side and I just wanted to be with him, right by his side. He was on his own. I was filled with dread for what I was about to see. When I was being wheeled there, I heard the ventilator.

Dear God, they must have nearly lost him.

He was in the oscillator.

The ventilator Ty had needed so badly. The ventilator Kyle hadn't needed but now did. Seeing him in this was too much. I barely remember the faces of the nurses and consultants, and forget the barrage of insults that flew from my mouth. I needed to get out of there. How the hell would we get through this? Was he going to live? What were we facing here? Another long day and night for sure.

That night I wrote:

Well Kyle, you gave us all a shock today and had everyone rushing round after you! Did you realise Ty wasn't next to you anymore? Was that why you took a turn for the worse? He will always be by your side, my darling; he will never leave you, not really. I believe he will always be with us all. Maybe in time he'll play some tricks and make you take the blame for his mischief! Watch out for that one! Your mummy will be watching and paying attention so closely to see if he tries to make us realise he's still there. Be a good boy, Kyle.

The lightness of my tone hid the fact that my heart was breaking and it only got worse.

Over the coming days, while Kyle fought for his life with us by his ventilator day and night, we had to think of Ty. I wrote to Kyle the day after we'd visited Ty in the mortuary – knowing his tiny body lay there killed both me and Tobias:

Mummy and Daddy went to visit Ty. He's now in an outfit that fits to keep him cosy, because he was always smaller than you. Ty is no longer in any pain Kyle, and hopefully one day we can sit you down and explain how you shared so much together. I hope you have the strength of two still – let's hope our little Ty fighter is cheering you on. He sacrificed so much, was in trouble inside my tum, gave everything to you, now you still have the opportunity to fight both corners. Hang in there pocket rocket!

Christmas was fast approaching, everything was winding up for the holidays and there was no way that our son was going to wait until New Year for us to plan his funeral. A wonderful woman called Jan had been coming in to help clean my room and had even offered to buy me some shopping, and as we got to know each other more over the days and weeks, she became a treasured friend and arranged for a funeral director to visit me in hospital. So, on Christmas Eve, Tobias carried a tiny white coffin holding a little miracle very close while our other little miracle lay full of tubes. Every part of him had something in or on him. As a mother, I didn't know where to be. I felt completely torn.

I wanted to be with Kyle, but I had to be there, to say goodbye to Ty, there was no other option really. I wasn't ready; I wasn't ready to let him go. The day he died, a part of me died too.

At the church, as Tobias stood up and spoke the eulogy, I barely knew where I was. Watching him hold Ty's tiny coffin had destroyed me. I was in such a daze but so proud that Tobias found the strength to stand up and speak. I heard the words, and they were beautiful, but how could my husband be speaking about our baby – how could this be happening?

As I look round this room today at all the close family and friends that have given up their Christmas Eve to be with us, I am reminded that none of you ever met my son. None of you ever had the chance. So, I would like to take this time to tell you who Ty was.

I first met Ty and his brother Kyle at their seven week scan. After getting over the shock of twins, I fell instantly in love with them. I have always wanted to be a dad and have honestly never felt so happy.

Unfortunately, our happiness was to be short-lived. At 16 weeks, we were told they were suffering from a life-threatening condition, twin-to-twin transfusion syndrome. The condition only affects identical twins and we soon found out how serious it was. Ty was not growing as fast as his brother; in short, Ty was giving his share of food to his brother and not getting enough for himself. The result of this was the need for hospital scans twice a week and it was in this time that we got to know his character. We tried everything to help our boys, from laser surgery to various other medical procedures.

Thanks to Amanda's bravery, courage and determination, we managed to get the boys to 29 weeks.

D Day came and I got the call every expectant father dreads – Ty was in trouble, his heart had started to fail. On the 16th of December, our boys were born.

We didn't even get to see them at that point as the doctors had to work fast.

Later that night I was finally introduced to my sons – I was so happy. I went to sleep that night, content and full of hope for the future, but, again, our happiness was to be short-lived. The next day the doctors told us they could not help Ty anymore.

Our little boy was dying.

Ty's last minutes were spent in his mum and dad's arms. I hope he knows how loved he is. Ty spent the little time he had fighting hard and giving selflessly to his brother. He truly was a hero. I'm so proud to be Ty's dad and can only imagine the kind of man he would have become with a character as strong as he showed. Hopefully, you now know him better and can always remember him as the beautiful baby boy he was.

I knew that everyone was in tears, and I was so grateful to those that were there. Many people had not turned up, people we thought we could rely on, people we thought would always be there for us – and, equally, there were other people who we never expected to be able to stand beside us that day, but they did. You truly do find out who your friends are at times like that.

I wrote in Kyle's diary that night:

Mummy and Daddy took Ty on a journey today; lots of people came to visit him too. Your baby brother is sleeping now and being loved by his granddad in heaven. Sleep tight little Ty fighter.

It was a living nightmare. I had said goodbye to my son and had no way of knowing whether I'd be saying goodbye to another.

It was made worse because straight after the service we moved into new accommodation elsewhere on the hospital grounds, meant to give us a bit more stability. But, with everything that the past few days had thrown at us, it only served to be unsettling, removing any previous comfort I had found. It was like being in another world, and being surrounded by many other heartbroken parents didn't help. One silver lining was a wonderful woman called Alison, a gutsy mum who I bounced off immediately and remain friends with to this day. We were both so broken and lost together; I couldn't have got through it without her support.

The day after the funeral was Christmas Day and I staggered through it.

Your first Christmas handsome! I think we'll wait until you are home safe and sound before we celebrate. Santa can come at other times of the year you know, he can always make exceptions for little stars like you. Daddy has gone home to make sure all your furry friends aren't up to mischief in their kennels. These are the names of your furry friends who you will share your home with – the huskies are Kuzak, Kamatz, Tzar, Cheeko, Cruise, Odin, Freya, Troy, Shimmer, Skeet, Cheeky, Thor, Hotfoot, Rocket, Valkryn, Maverick, Jet and Bullitt. They will all want to give you lots of licks and waggy tails! Who knows? Maybe you will follow in Mummy and Daddy's footsteps one day and race with some of these dogs? There's lots of fun in store for you, sweetheart.

Did I believe it? Did I believe the happy, optimistic lines I was spinning in the diary that all the nurses and doctors could read if they wanted to? I did and I didn't. I didn't expect any of what was happening; I couldn't think what the future might hold for Kyle now. Neither could I let all of my grief out as I still had Kyle to fight for, and I needed to hold onto the belief that he would pull through. They had, after all, said he had a 97% chance of survival to begin with and I clung onto that number. It was so hard. All our time was spent by Kyle's incubator and I was torn between needing to rest and recuperate myself, but also be there for my little man. At one point, a little baby girl was placed next to Kyle and I couldn't help but think, *that should have been Ty – he should be the one next to his brother.*

On the 29th of December, Kyle underwent surgery to put a clip on a valve that during pregnancy allows blood flow between the heart and lungs. For a full-term baby, the valve closes before birth but with premature babies that doesn't happen and it can be dangerous. We'd listened to other parents then being offered this procedure before their child's ventilation was changed, but Kyle hadn't been given that option, we'd never been given that option – it made us realise his ventilation should never have been changed so soon after birth and it could have explained some of the problems Kyle was having now. He should have been far more stable, had the clip and then changed ventilation. It was all so traumatic. The following day, his chest drain was taken out and he had a blood transfusion. But even though he seemed so small, we knew the operation was the only way to get Kyle breathing on his own and finally becoming stable. And soon after, we saw our first sign when Kyle managed to kick his little tootsies in the recovery room, which was marvellous to see. By New Year's Eve, I felt as if we'd been fighting forever.

Well Kyle, this is a Christmas and New Year we never thought you'd see considering we expected you and Ty to still be all tucked up in Mummy's tummy. You made a big impact on 2008, I wrote to him.

The doctors were pushing him to breathe on his own now and by the first day of the year, they got the tube out of his mouth and put him on something called C-Pap ventilation. He was built like a little Action Man; he was so little and watching blood being taken from his foot was so hard, I often had to leave the room. But my baby bear was doing so well.

This is another big day for you, Kyle – you had your milk increased to 5ml per hour and your arterial line removed. We got lots of lovely pictures of us all having cuddles, I told him on the 2 January. *You're a tad tired tonight but keep up the good work!*

By the next day, he was up to 8ml. His antibiotics were being reduced and the tubes taken away. *Keep fighting,* I told him, *it shouldn't be a problem . . . it's in your genes!* He then went up to 9ml an hour and there were finally no nasty needles or lines in his tiny little veins. He looked like a little person by now – a real baby boy, and on the 4 January, I was finally able to hold him in my arms for the first time. As I lay him on my chest, I buttoned my big, baggy shirt around him in a little cocoon so he'd be warm and feel my heart beat. It was a magical moment.

Kyle was still in the smallest size nappies and we joked that he was like a little Simon Cowell, because they almost came up to his chin! But I truly felt that the finishing line was in sight. By the time he and Ty would have been 32 weeks, so 3 weeks old on the outside, Kyle was sucking on his dummy and managing to push it back in when it popped out. The doctors told me how advanced that was – is it any wonder that I had such hope? He also looked as if he was laughing a lot of the time, but surely he was too little for that? 'Are those just special smiles for Mummy?' I asked him, and thought of the days when we would laugh and run about together.

There were lots of highs and lows – one day we were finally able to put him in these special babygros that had openings for all his tubes, the next he needed another blood transfusion. Tobias was still having to deal with everything in Inverness and come down to Glasgow when he could, and all of our friends were amazing and mucking in with the dogs.

By the middle of January, we'd seen a huge improvement. *Well handsome,* I wrote, *what a long way you've come in a month. Right now, mummy's sitting beside you while you're all cosy and completely unaware of the blizzard outside.* Kyle had his first bath at that point which seemed a huge achievement.

What a journey this first month of your little life has been so far. Both you and Ty battled not to be so sick while inside Mummy's tummy, but staying in the warmth was not an option – an early appearance was all you could do. Your brother had to fight that little bit harder inside and out, but we think he did that just to be with us all even if it was only for a short while – 26 hours to be exact. Ty will always be with us and probably stick even closer to you, Kyle. Side by side always. You, on the other hand, are still battling – don't ease up when you see the finish in sight, run straight through and don't go slower until you're past it, handsome. We are so very proud of you and what you've achieved so far, keep the pace going. We love you little guy!

When it finally came time to move Kyle out of the Intensive Care Unit and on to the Special Care Baby Unit, I felt an odd conflict of emotions. Of course I wanted him to progress, but that was the room where he had been beside Ty, a room with all those memories. I was torn.

That door's closed, I wrote. *It's the room your brother lay next to you after you made your impacts into this*

world and into our hearts. And in that room we did
the hardest but kindest thing we could ever do for Ty.
But now, little guy, it's time for you to spread your tiny
wings and go for it.

Kyle gave us such a fright the next day when he was taken out of the ICU because he immediately took a turn for the worse – however, his space was taken immediately and there were no beds left in the ICU, so he had to be moved to the surgical ward. He was full of drama this one! When we called the next day, on the morning of the 27 January, we were told that he had been terribly sick overnight and they had had to make room for him in the ICU. It was awful and I couldn't help but feel he hadn't been the same since they'd moved him.

When Kyle did finally leave the ICU for good on the 5 February and headed to the Special Baby Care Unit, I gave a little sniffle as I thought of Ty and said 'goodbye' once more. This time, Kyle wouldn't be back there. The nurses in ICU had a special term for those doing well, saying they're 'One step closer to the door', meaning they're one step closer to freedom.

My boy was on the way – we were over the worst.

With Kyle getting more stable by the day, I began to think outside the bubble of his hospital room. I had to go to Inverness at one point to check on the progress of the new house. We'd wanted everything done by the time our boys arrived but now we were struggling with what we'd taken on. Tobias was exhausted and it was such a hard time, but I was in panic mode – I had no control over my boys and it didn't help that I was feeling like I had no control over the house or the dogs either. The little things affected me more than usual too – I found it so hard letting go of the reins, so I just did what I could do. And what I could do then was take a few days out to make sure the house was well on the way to being ready for my little man. His nursery even had its own en suite which was hilarious, given that a basin was too big for his baths at the moment! The house was shaping up nicely, so I only needed to stay away for two days but I missed him so much. The nurses had encouraged me to go out and look at some nice baby things for Kyle, maybe just to give me a bit of hope. But all I remember is standing in Mothercare feeling completely overwhelmed and lost. I had originally planned to buy for two, now I just needed things for one. But however hard I found it, I knew how important it was for me to get through it.

I also suffered a tragic loss at the time; Odin, my best friend, sadly passed away on my trip home and it was horrific. He came up to me and rested his chin on my feet as I sat in a rocking chair that Tobias's dad had made for me to nurse Kyle. Then suddenly he went outside and collapsed. I lost him that night at 2am. It was like he'd waited for me to come home before he gave in. I was almost numb to the pain, not thinking I could take anymore. But remembering Odin's peaceful strength and his love and loyalty spurred me on once more . . .

Kyle was still getting transfusions, but he was putting on weight so there were not too many worries. It was steady. My guilt from being away from the dogs still preyed on me, particularly knowing they'd be feeling the loss of Odin, and every time something popped up to remind me of my other life, it felt even worse.

Today it's the big Aviemore sled dog race, I wrote to my little boy. *We should have been there if Mummy got her way and you and Ty had stayed put. We've won that race before but this time all the dogs back home will have to sit it out. If we don't tell them, they won't make a fuss! I can't wait for you to meet them, Kyle; they're going to love you and accept you as their own, and as one of the pack. You're going to have such a great life.*

I breastfed my baby for the first time that day and he took to it like a husky to a harness. *That's all you have to do, little guy – just get strong,* I told him. Although the next day he wasn't so keen, all his tests were perfect. When he was naughty (which meant he wasn't cooperating with the nurses), I would use one of my favourite phrases on him: *if you're going to run with the big dogs, you can't wee like a puppy!* And he never let me down . . .

CHAPTER 7

Part of the pack

In those first few months of Kyle's life between ICU and the Special Baby Care Unit we saw improvements then setbacks back and forth. In ICU, he sustained a burn from medication leaking onto his skin from tubes and his veins became exhausted from having bloods taken. In fact, when the light shone on Kyle's body you could see dots everywhere, representing all the needles that had searched for blood, all the tubes that had been stuck in his little body. And when he was back in the Special Baby Care Unit for good, he also had to have another operation to remove a small cyst from his throat that at first they thought was scar tissue ... as if he hadn't already gone through enough.

We became obsessed with the numbers on the monitors, what was good, what was bad. We spent so much time with the fabulous nurses who made you feel at ease, knowing they'd carry out anything necessary and in the calmest and most caring ways while you needed to try and sleep. Of course we had our favourites and still stay in touch even now.

I think back to that first Christmas and New Year that was spent by Kyle's side with great fondness in some ways, as we tried to raise a smile or two with the staff whilst watching the fireworks bring in 2009. I keep going back to that – to the start of the year the boys should have been born.

I kept going with the diary, which was proving to be something of therapy for me. I could write my views or any feelings I had in there which was really cathartic. I was the only one to write in the diary and have kept it private, scared to open those memories to this day. Writing this now, I'm facing memories that I'd subconsciously put in a memory box in my mind. I really felt we'd been dealt such a bad hand but forging on was the only way to move forward. There was nothing else for it.

We learned harsh lessons and those lessons certainly helped me see people for what they really are. And I promised myself I'd make it up to the dogs I felt I had neglected. It wasn't by choice but I know they wondered where I was. I missed flying through the forest trails with them pulling me at a hell of a pace, their breath in the cold air and the sound of their breathing. I wanted to get out of myself and back into a routine. They were the most loyal friends of all who had got me through so much and I knew we were all going to need them a lot from hereon in too. I had to make things up to them in times to come.

Kyle spent another few weeks on the Special Care Baby Unit in Glasgow before being finally being transferred to a hospital in Inverness, the final stepping stone. We spent those few weeks visiting him round the clock while we got the house ready and dust-free. He'd fought so hard to live and this little miracle was going to make it. He was near to the finish line and I was so proud of him.

For the first six months of his little life he spent it in hospitals on machines keeping him alive. His journey was finally bringing him home but we had so much to take in. We had a huge family that was growing all the time and Kyle was just part of that pack. I had always dreamed that he would be welcomed by the dogs as a new puppy, and that is just what happened. They were all so gentle with him as if they understood that the usual rules didn't apply. They backed off when they needed to, and accepted that he made strange noises or grabbed at them sometimes when they went past.

The rescue dogs we have are all very protective anyway, but I felt this even more so with Kyle. I do think they want to protect us desperately – who knows whether that is because they know what we have saved them from or whether they would do it no matter their owner, but I never feel scared or vulnerable when my boys and girls are around. Just as Kyle is the puppy in their pack, I am part of that pack too. I would do anything for them and I feel they would do anything for us as well. It's actually a very beautiful thing to have such a bond, and I know we are blessed – I just hope that no one ever tries to get between me and any of my dogs, or they would no doubt pay the price one way or another!

What's even funnier is the fact that the rescue dogs that have joined this very large canine family seemed to have perfected the art of howling. Taught by the best teachers really! I remember sitting on the terrace of a village pub nearby on a summer's night, having a quick G&T for the road, and I could hear my pack at home. I got really teary – it was as if they were all calling, *come home now, mumma!*

It's such a haunting sound with some howls in particular that just captivate you. I can pick out who's who from a pack howl just as you could identify your family or friends from their voices in a crowd. It's just as haunting to me when we've lost dogs to illness or old age and miss the contribution they made to the pack howls. The howls take place for many reasons – a social song after breakfast is always a sure thing. When you leave the house, even just to take another dog for a walk, they call on you. Their reactions also alert you to different things – I know when to respond and when to ignore, just like I've had to learn what Kyle needs and when. Sometimes it is wildlife that sets the dogs off given that we live in a very rural scenic part of Scotland but when it's a human nearby, they make a completely different noise. I always trust the dogs and if they're not happy with people hanging around and adopt a particular stance, then I'm not happy either.

The very first husky we got, who introduced us to the unconventional life we now live was a master at oozing presence and he had the most remarkable howls. Kuzak was affectionately known as Uncle Kuz or, in latter years, The Old Man. He projected authority with his calm, confident no-nonsense approach to life and earned his title of 'Uncle' Kuz through taking the other rescue dogs under his wise protective wing. So when someone nosed around our property they were very wary of this almost-magical white male who simply sat and watched. I never discouraged that. The fact he wasn't capable of taking on any intruder was a different matter but his silence spoke volumes. And there were others in the kennel that would have obliged quite happily if an attack was required!

When the time came for the old man to leave us, just two weeks before his 16th year, we laid him to rest beside his pack members who had gone before him. I placed a rose in beside him and a few lines as a farewell letter as I've done time and time again, only this time the whole kennel erupted into the most haunting howl as we stood and sobbed. They were bidding him farewell too. He played such a massive part in keeping peace with the rescue crew. He'd patrol the dog playground, just enjoying his twilight years, and could muster up the occasional trot to play a little. So these days his howl, one that bellowed from within the pack, is very much missed.

As the years had gone by, the canine crew grew and, naturally, we had lost some of our older dogs. Khandi was around 16 years old when she passed in 2003, before we were even married. The day she died was horrific for us – we never realised just how big a part she played in the pack until she was gone. One of our huskies, Odin, cradled her basket nuzzling her to wake up. It was soul-destroying to see and, for a while, he warned off her two other friends who wanted to bid her farewell, one of them being the pack leader, Kuzak.

Those three boys sat on her grave for two days in the rain. It was hard to watch. At that point, we realised Khandi was Alpha female to them. Odin was such a sensitive dog; I was convinced he was human in a former life. He was so intuitive and could read me like a book. How was it possible for a dog to be so switched on, I often wondered? He certainly was though – losing him in 2009 tore me apart. In fact, every time I lose a canine member of my family they take a part of me with them – at this rate, there won't be anything left.

Dogs really are amazing. Just watching, observing teaches you so much. I've not really read much on behaviour or training dogs other than what I've picked up over the years. I'm sure I'm wrong in many situations but I've learned a hell of a lot from my own dogs. We've never really taught dogs to sit, roll over or beg or do tricks. My training methods have involved teaching sled dogs to run, to pull and be good at it. As the years have gone by, we've grown to 40 strong. With our kennel of Siberian huskies and Scandinavian hounds, our racing sled dogs are now competing at international level. We've won medals at international competitions such as the IFSS Dryland Sled Dog World Championships in Borken, Germany and it's occasions like that which make me so proud of those canine athletes who are a huge part of our family and our way of life. I always think that the rescue dogs are the cheerleaders among the pack – they maybe couldn't do what the sled dogs do, but they're an invaluable part of our team.

And Kyle was part of that team.

As Kyle grew, it was evident to others that he wasn't hitting the goals he should, which wasn't really as clear to us as first time parents. I'd started to notice things, as a mother, from around 6 months, little things. Not being able to turn over or crawl, for example. There were often remarks from other mothers and not always the most tactful of comments. We pushed for answers to our questions yet nobody really seemed willing to commit to what was going on. It made everything so much harder. Kyle had left the hospital on home oxygen, something I found it difficult to deal with, and he was still using it now. I was scared and don't mind admitting that, but there has never been any support for feeling that way, any recognition that what we and Kyle are going through is hard.

One thing Kyle was capable of was pulling out the nasal prongs from his nose and keeping us on our toes rushing to put them back in place. I always felt happier watching the numbers on his monitor get back to figures we were happy with, but it was a constant battle.

At around seven months old, he had another little cyst in his throat that inhibited him taking solids. It was just like the one he had when he was in Glasgow too when he'd had to have an operation at only a few weeks old. There just seemed like there were setbacks throughout – we expected some, but we wanted to know what was wrong other than his prematurity presenting delayed development. So we asked if he could be tested to determine whether or not it was time to come off oxygen. Again, we seemed to be presented with a non-committal response so I asked for him to be seen by the team in Glasgow who brought him into the world. They agreed to do what is known as a sleep study, with Kyle being linked up to wires and machines monitoring how he handled breathing in his sleep without help. I had a feeling he could nail this but what I was hit with on that trip tore my world apart . . . again.

CHAPTER 8

Fighting

I remember vividly the day Kyle was assessed in Glasgow a few months later as he crawled – or tried to crawl – around the floor playing with hospital toys. I caught one or two of those oh-so-familiar looks I'd seen before throughout my pregnancy when there was a problem.

'Aren't you a clever boy?' I said to him, over and over, every time he achieved something. Kyle was clever to me – he was a miracle.

As usual, no one said anything to me other than platitudes as it all went on. I felt as if it was me and my boy against the world.

After the assessment I got him settled into the ward where the sleep study would take place that night. I'd sleep right by his side. I wouldn't leave him; I'd be by his side until my last breath.

My head was racing as I took in the events of the day. Something had happened in the ward that would be an indicator of Kyle's condition later down the road and at the time had me in fits of laughter. I had no idea what it really meant. The child in the bed adjacent to Kyle had visitors that evening and each time they moved a chair, it screeched along the hospital floor. Well, he just laughed so heartily that the whole ward joined in. You could see he was getting tired from laughing so hard as it was going through his whole body. That night the smile was soon wiped off my face when I was paid a visit from the consultant present at the arrival of the twins, the same consultant who came to tell us Ty was dying and who was also present at the assessment that day. She was a very gently spoken woman and was searching to find the right words.

There were no right words.

It was sure to hit me like a train. She told me that Kyle had some motor skill problems.

'What were they?' I asked.

This is where the hospital red tape came in, rules and regulations, jurisdiction because we lived in the Scottish Highlands now. She was not allowed to tell me and she wouldn't tell me. I felt sick and burst into tears. I was presented with a problem I was trying to resolve in my head while my brain was in a 500mph frenzy trying to fathom what the term meant. *Motor skill problems.* She held my hand, telling me she never saw this coming for Kyle. Never thought this was on the cards and that she knew someone very close to her who had a child with difficulties.

The room spun around me. I was alone as Kyle lay beside me. Did this have anything to do with him haemorrhaging when he was taken off ventilation? How the hell did I break this to his Daddy? I felt so angry that I was again faced with something to fight – when would we catch a break? I had to make that call to Tobias whilst hoping I could keep a panic attack at bay, something I'd experienced twice before. How do you make a call saying something is wrong with our son but they won't tell me what? But that's pretty much what I had to do. Tobias came to collect us and we left the hospital wondering how our lives had turned out this way.

It was 5 November and by the time we arrived home the village bonfire was in full swing. I felt as if we were in the middle of something that was burning as fast and furious as those flames, something that was out of control and we just had to go with.

The months drifted by whilst our local hospital sat on a diagnosis. It was well into the next year – we'd celebrated Kyle's second birthday and were closer to his third – before we finally sat in a room with another nine people waiting to hear what they had decided about our son; we finally got to the root of what we were dealing with.

Kyle had been diagnosed with cerebral palsy.

Our little boy played on the floor while each of the specialists had their say as they told us he would never lead a normal life, that his brain damage was too severe, that he would never reach the milestones we hoped for. We'd been told to expect initial development delays but no one had ever prepared us for a diagnosis like this. To have to press for a diagnosis then get hit smack in the face with it was bad enough, but to be told in a crowded room just felt so wrong, so impersonal.

We didn't realise it at the time but when we walked out of that room, our lives had changed forever. From then on, we had a constant flow of health professionals through the house, talking at us. Given that they had failed *both of* my boys and treated us so badly, I was so unwilling to trust them with my son's condition. It was such a horrible time. I had always wanted a career and a family – now, I was expected to sit back and listen to these people, not question anything and it all felt like I was slowly losing control. I just couldn't resign myself and my family to that life.

When you have a child with additional special needs, your life changes beyond all recognition. One of the first things you learn is that you have very little privacy. Your days are either lonely and isolated as you struggle on with little, or no, help, or they are filled with strangers asking questions, doing tests, filling out paperwork. I found those days very hard to deal with as I felt that I was the only one who really knew what life with Kyle was really like, not the pen pushers who surrounded us at every opportunity.

For the next few years of Kyle's life, Tobias and I were part of a mad upside-down world where people who didn't live with Kyle, didn't love Kyle, rode roughshod over what we knew was best for him. It was always about whether they could tick a box, not whether the decision was the right one for our son. We were part of a scary new world and we were learning just how little control we had over it.

Kyle's cerebral palsy and severe brain damage didn't make any difference to me – he was still my baby and I would do all I could for him, but I would be lying if I said it was easy. Just as fertility problems can break a couple, so can having a child with difficulties. I desperately needed to still be 'me' not just the carer of a boy like Kyle, but I know that there were times when my marriage was close to breaking.

Tobias and I were under such strain. He would head off to work and I would be at home with Kyle and the dogs. His job wasn't easy, he had plenty of stresses, but there were moments that I envied him. He got out, he got a life. When he came back, I would have a list of things I wanted to talk to him about – sometimes I wouldn't have seen another adult all day, or I would only have been dealing with bureaucrats. It was hard for both of us, and I think we did lose our way a little.

Kyle didn't have any language that could really be understood by people outside the family, and he certainly couldn't walk or move about by himself but I was determined that he would go to school, and have as normal a life as possible. Still, many people thought I was mad – and why wouldn't they? We don't really integrate in our society, we see the Kyles of the world as a problem. I remember Tobias once asking a health professional why we didn't see adults like Kyle around – he was told that was because they were all locked away in institutions. That will never happen to my boy. He fought tooth and nail to be here and I will never give up on him.

I knew I had to think of a way to settle our family and also drive my ambition forward.

This became my focus. I wouldn't rot; I wouldn't let my boy be failed by a mother who did nothing and so couldn't be there for him in every way he needed. Or like those mothers who have no support network and are beaten down by the system. Not me. I have a saying that goes, 'throw me to the wolves and I'll come back leading the pack'. Well, I wanted the world to take notice, and I wanted to make a difference.

Despite Kyle's life-changing prognosis, he was a happy boy. He loved playing alone, happy in his little world with friends that spoke to him – his teddies. The ones that flashed lights and sang to him; he was so motivated by those toys. What we couldn't work out was his obsession with creaking doors. It quickly became a fixation to open and close the doors on the TV cabinet until it screeched. If you oiled it, he would keep doing the same thing until it screeched again. He loved silly noises as I assumed most kids did but other people were seeing something more in this than we realised. He was developing many little habits. Like playing with the same toy over and over, nothing else. The lights and sounds played a huge role in it all, so much repetition, just like the noises that tickled him back in the hospital as the chairs screeched along the rubber floors. It was all so funny to him.

We were so grateful that Kyle could entertain himself, and we were also lucky to find him a place at a local nursery that catered for his needs and gave him 1-on-1 attention. And as we learned more about his condition we were able to move to a more suitable school that supported his particular needs; it was definitely a relief.

With this extra support, it meant I could try to find that something for me. I'd always been interested in animal rescue, as you know, but recently had taken in three dogs from abroad. Scarlett was our first, in 2012, rescued from barbaric conditions in Romania.

It was becoming a bigger and bigger part of my life and as the months went by, we settled into our little routine, the dogs, Kyle and us. Kyle was locked in a world without siblings, but he had a family of dogs who, though they have no real connections, all love him unconditionally. In fact, the dogs have more compassion and patience than most humans I know!

I'd never put my son in harm's way and did my research very carefully before bringing rescue dogs into the mix, and they have blown me away with their compassion, love, patience and tolerance of one another despite some horrifically disturbing backgrounds.

I've often found it amazing to see the look on health professionals' faces as they wince disapprovingly about the relationships between a boy with Kyle's conditions and his canine family. But I truly believe that some of those dogs are more intelligent than people. If my dog or dogs don't approve of someone it's normally with good reason and I'm more inclined to take note of that. They're very good judges of character and if your scent smells weird to them they sense trouble, you're not welcome and I'm less likely to trust you.

I remember one health visitor in particular (one of the many; that lack of continuity added to our problems too – they always seemed to be changing jobs or planning to retire!). She visited and gave me advice on feeding solids that I knew made Kyle vomit, despite me telling her what he would tolerate. I did chuckle when she berated me for saying Kyle's claws needed to be clipped – she reminded me he wasn't a dog!

In fact, there's always so much reference to Kyle's weight – him being thin, not reaching milestones. We beat ourselves up trying to make sure his meals were carefully planned, as long as he enjoyed it . . . and he did! Chicken, roast potatoes gravy – he loved them. But because other carers found feeding him difficult we were encouraged to use a gastrostomy tube to supplement his diet. After we did our own research, we were really worried because it risked affecting what Kyle could take orally but again, we were told it was the right thing for him. What would you have done? Within a week of the surgery, Kyle had stopped drinking and eating completely – everything we feared was happening in front of our eyes. From then on, we had a battle on our hands – the more agile and strong Kyle got, the more difficulties we faced. We'd find him swinging a 500ml pack of high calorie milk that was attached to his tummy, it was so dangerous and we had to sleep with one eye open and even set up a video monitor in his room so we could make sure he didn't hurt himself during the night. Naturally, he lost weight and was really skinny during this time – it was like we were all on a runaway train with no way of jumping off!

We have really experienced ups and downs. The saying, 'too many cooks spoil the broth' is pretty much spot on. You have a group of health professionals busting heads adding 2 and 2 and getting 22. One meeting regarding Kyle has always stayed with me and it was a big turning point for the family – in fact, we had a discussion with people involved in his care who we felt were downright wrong and even questioned our ability to care for Kyle. These were people who we were meant to trust but it appeared to us that it was an exercise in exuding authority over us; we knew we were within our rights to feel the way we did and, in our opinion, this wasn't standard practice. My own mother worked with disabled children for over 20 years, Tobias's mother is an additional support needs teacher and we have another family member who sits on a children's panel – seeing the reactions of these people in the room in front of me, people who I felt were attempting to pull the wool over our eyes and everyone around them, was extremely uncomfortable. Well, we certainly made our opinions clear after that and I'll never forget it. I remember a particular person in the room who sat there with quivering cheeks, as if even they realised we were being treated unfairly. It was horrific.

In such a serious moment, I couldn't help but find the humour in someone trying to exude authority and arrogance while having a dirty toenail poking through their shoe! That someone whose job needed to be so structured, have the minutest attention to detail could pay such little attention to detail in their own personal care was a real surprise. To me, it was as vile as their actions made me feel that day. But focussing on that distracted me emotionally I guess and it's helped me to cope a few other times over the last few years.

The first few years of Kyle's life were tough; watching a little boy fight so hard to live dealing with things us adults would really struggle with broke my heart. Babies, although fragile, are much tougher than we give them credit for, but it was when he got a bit older that I really found it difficult to watch.

We have always been aware that Kyle is on the autistic spectrum. We have never had much eye contact from him, but, as the years went by, this fact became more and more obvious. You can only lie to yourself for so long but now he could go to school it couldn't be ignored. I told myself every excuse under the sun – maybe he was looking more when I was doing something else, maybe he just didn't like to make such contact with anyone, maybe this, maybe that. The truth of the matter was, it became ever more apparent that there was next to no visual contact happening between Kyle and anyone else. People often ask 'how do you cope?' I know they mean well, I know that they are trying to be sympathetic but I don't want to dwell on it. How do I cope? I just do, I have to.

If someone had laid out my life in front of me and told me what would happen with my babies, I would have wondered how I'd cope too. Yes, there are people living golden lives, but there are also those struggling more than anyone will ever know. They just cope too. You get on with things. You only look ahead when you have the strength to do so. And, above all, you cling on to every bit of positivity there is.

With Kyle, I love what he loves. If he gets enjoyment from something, I do too. I don't let myself think that he should be riding a bike by now, that I should be giving him a ticking off for eating too many sweets or not doing his homework. I just thank my lucky stars that he's still with us. From the start, he has always loved watching the dogs walk around. The bushy tails on the huskies have made him laugh from when he was a tiny little thing, so that made me and Tobias laugh too. Those little moments are what keep you going – the little lights in the dark. Kyle's love of dogs has obviously come from us, it was in his bones, and I should have guessed it would come out in some way. However, because we had so little to cling on to, any sign of interest or engagement meant a huge amount. When he was a baby, and still on oxygen, he would laugh so much while his eyes followed Troy, one of our incredibly fast Siberian huskies, around the room.

'What is he finding so hysterical?' I would ask Tobias, as we both joined in the laughter.

'No idea,' he'd reply, 'but as long as something makes him happy, who cares?'

After a while we noticed exactly what it was.

'Look! It's Troy's tail!' Sure enough, that was exactly what was sending our little boy into fits of happiness. Every time our daft dog wagged his bushy tail close to Kyle, the laughter would increase. It went round in circles because the more Kyle laughed, the more Troy wagged! The dog would trot around the room, wagging and wagging, swishing his bushy tail from side to side, as Kyle got more and more worked up with delight too. In fact, there were times he would get so excited that he would make himself sick.

'Ah, never mind,' I'd tell him, wiping it up, 'being happy is what matters.' Another bit of cleaning never bothered me; it was just all part of a normal day as Kyle's mum. The thing was, and I know I've said this before, but I really had never thought of myself as maternal, even though Tobias had always assured me I was. But now that I had a child, I would have fought for him to the death.

It's hard trying to avoid dwelling on all the things your child misses out on when they have needs like Kyle. I knew that he would never do such simple things such as go out on his own to the park, get into trouble for breaking his curfew, hang around with his friends instead of revising for exams, and it broke my heart. He can't join in with the other kids, no parties, no sleepovers; it is hard to see. I try to focus on the positives – he is loved and he is safe. As long as Tobias and I were around, he always would be. However, you can't help but think of the future, of what will happen when you aren't around. I try to block that out, but I know it is something Tobias thinks about a lot.

Seeing Kyle react to the dogs was always wonderful but it was rare. They all adored him, but he didn't have a particular favourite – I think they were just part of the furniture to him.

'What you need,' I said to him one day, 'is a special friend.'

I had no idea that there was one out there, just waiting for him . . .

CHAPTER 9

Finding Miracle

It was an ordinary day in May 2013 and I was scrolling through a social media animal rescue page, something which was now part of my daily routine. Every morning, once I'd showered, got Kyle off to school, the dogs sorted, and felt as if I could take five minutes, I was accustomed to quickly checking the pages of a number of groups. I'd see their news, find out what they were up to, and hope that I'd read about a forever home being found for a street or shelter dog.

After that dreadful day when Kyle was assessed, that determination to have a life for not only Kyle, but for me and Tobias too, had built up inside me. There are a lot of good people out there and, although these pages showed the horrors that are inflicted on innocent creatures, they also restored my faith in human nature. For some people, there was no limit to what they would do to rescue a dog that had captured their heart.

I knew the feeling all too well – my home was now filled with dogs I'd saved as well as the sled dogs, and I didn't doubt for a second that there would be another one day. Not just now though. Life was frantic to say the least, but I would and could help in other ways, whether it was fundraising or putting people in touch with each other, so my daily routine continued and I began looking through the pages.

One of the people I followed with interest was a woman who lived in Thailand called Bitter (Bee) Brownie. I had huge admiration for her from the moment I'd first found out about her work. She was heavily involved in rescuing street dogs, someone who selflessly and on a regular basis gave up her time to embark on dog rescue missions around Thailand. In fact, she'd not only saved 3 of mine but she had saved hundreds of others, helping them eventually reach adoptive families around the world. She was fearless and tireless; goodness knows how many she had led to new families who cherished them, but there were an awful lot of dogs out there who owed their lives to this indefatigable woman. I had looked at a few pages that fateful morning in May and thought I'd keep Bitter Brownie's until last, desperately hoping there would be an uplifting tale.

Then, in a flash, while browsing through her photos came the moment that changed my life; that changed the lives of so many.

In front of me was an image that sent shockwaves through my entire body. I felt electrified. My heart, my head, my very soul were touched by the dog on my screen as soon as I saw it. I didn't know if it was a boy or a girl. I didn't even know if it was dead or alive.

I just saw the picture.

In front of me was an almost-lifeless scrap, head and front leg dangling through a rusty old cage packed with other dogs, all suffering. This inert, limp, scabby, broken soul had at some point made a last bid for freedom by forcing through the rusty sharp cages that clearly had been used time and again to carry dogs. You could see the damage that had been caused, the scars and the cuts. As the camera flashed, the dog had opened one eye, a sign of life in all that horror and, with that one gesture, I felt a connection.

Hard hitting, powerful, it captivated me in an instant.

They all break your heart but there was something about this one that was sending shivers down my spine. This dog was in a terrible way but there was a beauty there; a majesty that had not yet been beaten. The very fact that there was still a spark that allowed a break for freedom to be attempted, spoke volumes.

I wasn't the only one who had seen Bitter Brownie's post. That photo broke hearts around the world that day and it certainly broke mine. It had me captivated to the point I didn't even immediately read the information saying whether this dog was actually alive. Seeing a powerful photo like this tears your heart apart but for those animals . . . they were on a truck that would be reeking of death, bound for an unspeakable hell. I knew what world this dog had been born into; in fact, nowadays, thanks to social media, many do. Lots of people are aware of the dog meat trade which originates in Thailand but it happens in lots of other countries too, which needs a lot more attention. Dogs – many of them pets, some street dogs, some from temples and other places of worship – are lured and captured by heartless traders, packed into cages with dozens and dozens of others, and transported to their death, to be eaten in Vietnam. That death is neither quick nor humane. The dog I was looking at was going through torture, but there was more of it to come – if life wasn't already over.

I couldn't tear my eyes form the screen. This dog's head was just hanging there. It had clearly been desperate to find an escape route and hung motionless, defeated by its attempt and cowed into submission. Whilst bearing the weight of other broken souls lying on top with nowhere to go, move or reposition, this was nothing less than a circle of Hell for these animals. With a combination of exhaustion and starvation, time was clearly running out, or had already. In fact, many around the world thought on the first glimpse that Bee (as Bitter Brownie was known to her supporters) had photographed what she presumed was another dead dog.

But . . . that flash of her camera had caused the dog to open an eye and the photo which showed that tiny movement changed everything. *If there was life then, I wondered, could it still be there? Could that spark be carrying this traumatised soul even further?*

I remember that day vividly. With tears flowing down my face and dropping from my chin, I couldn't comprehend how this dog wasn't dead – nor could I explain the feeling I had that it was *still* alive. *You're still there, aren't you?* I whispered to the screen. *You're still with us.* At this point, I commented on the rescue page it was a miracle. For me, the name stuck and was perfectly suited to this little dog.

I couldn't stop thinking about what I'd seen all day. As I went about looking after our other dogs – quite a task as we had thirty-seven at that point – and doing various household chores and things relating to our restaurant business, I was always thinking about the miracle dog. I chatted to him in my mind – and sometimes out loud – for the rest of the morning and afternoon.

I knew that Bee would be posting further updates when she had them and I had to be very strict with myself to stop from checking her page constantly but, when lunchtime rolled round, I started up my laptop again and looked immediately. The dogs she had pictured in the crates had all been saved after their huge truck was intercepted. I was told that the men who were transporting them had run off – while it isn't illegal to eat dog in Thailand, it is against the law to slaughter or transport them there. It's a complicated system of different rules in each country, from Thailand to Vietnam to the Philippines to China to India to Laos to Cambodia. In some areas, it is the skin that is of high value, being used for drum kits, for example, in others for meat, in others for delicacies. Skin from dogs' testicles is exported to Japan to make golf gloves, if you can believe it. Many even believe that if the dog is tortured, the meat is tastier – this appalling attitude results in dogs being tortured and starved and beaten, sometimes killed in vats of boiling water, generally skinned alive or sometimes blowtorched to death, all because of some ridiculous notion that the adrenalin which courses through their veins due to these practices makes tougher flesh, making men more virile.

It was a miraculous rescue – the group of volunteers had managed to rescue all of those they had found in the crates from this lorry load, but I had no idea which ones were still alive, or which ones had died since the photos were taken. The task to remove the dogs was underway but it was not an easy one when there were hundreds of broken souls with broken limbs too. Sometimes they even tie the dogs' front legs behind their back, so they suffer horribly on the journeys. I soon found out that many had already given up, many had died. These trips can see dogs on board for days without water in unbearable heat. In this case, it was heart wrenching that so many had lost their lives so close to freedom – although I did think that, had circumstances been different and the truck had reached its destination, then it was a blessing they had taken their last breaths before the sheer horrors that awaited them.

Those trucks are on a one-way trip and no one shows mercy. The sad reality is that there are so many cages on most trips that cranes are used to remove the cages, with dogs packed in as tight as sardines in a tin. Gradually, they're lowered to the ground where it's all hands on deck to remove them. It is almost impossible to comprehend the fear they must feel. After being captured, sometimes from loving homes, they are then treated with nothing but brutality so they don't understand they've been rescued and are now safe. Some may lash out to protect themselves if they have any energy left at all, but most are browbeaten.

Once free from the cages they stagger, some can't move through being bound so long; they are broken spirits, broken limbs, surrounded by piles of death. They don't even realise they're safe now.

Among the photos of Bee's rescue lay the dog I was now inexplicably bound to, lowered to the ground but still confined with the others, all tightly packed. I breathed a sigh of relief on seeing a relatively alert looking head as I searched through the pictures, but would this be short-lived? Could this dog actually make it? Or would it be so riddled with the diseases that spread through dogs like a wildfire in such close confinement? Only time would tell.

Come on, I urged, *don't give up! Hold on in there and I'll help, I'll do everything I can to find you a home, just keep fighting little one!*

That truck had never made it to Vietnam but sadly the smugglers made frequent trips – this little guy might have been rescued (hopefully), but there was a seemingly never-ending stream of dogs being exploited and tortured. I knew of 2 or 3 interceptions around that time but the smugglers were relentless. These heartless bastards would continue to steal people's pets and catch as many street dogs as they could. I had been told in the past that those who consume dog meat will pay more to eat pedigree, so I knew that it wasn't just strays that were being taken. The aim was just to get the cargo into the hands of butchers as quickly as possible. From Thailand, others can even travel further to China where more can be earned for their pounds of flesh.

As I've learned more, it only gets worse. There are various sickening methods used to kill but torture is always high on the list. I've seen footage of dogs reaching the butchers where if they're too thin they are force fed before trade. Their helpless limbs hog tied, a tube is forced down their throats pumping them full of dry rice or even stones. As if that's not bad enough, water is then hosed down their throats, all adding instant weight before their mouths can be bound shut. All this happens in front of other animals – can you imagine that fear, knowing you're next? They're also skinned alive while conscious. But this is what those barbaric cold and calculating individuals thrive on – fear. The more adrenalin that is pumping through their bodies, the better the flesh will taste, or so they believe. I can't even politely put into words just how angry this makes me, the rage that boils inside of me when I think of them taking so much pleasure inflicting so much pain.

Since knowing of this trade it has consumed me. Knowing what these animals endure is haunting – I know it is hard to read about, but we are their only voice. By staying quiet, by turning the other way through feeling upset or not being able to look at images on social media, we sadly solve nothing. They continue to suffer unless we put aside our feelings and remember who is really suffering. Everyone needs a voice, be them human or animal. I am no different to anyone else, I feel sick seeing the most graphic images and videos but in order to push for changes and fight for those helpless animals I have to remember one important thing – my emotions need to be swept under the rug. It doesn't matter how upset I am – I'm not being torn limb from limb, they are.

Culture is one thing, and I do try to understand that people have different beliefs, but when it comes to barbaric torture, I'm not convinced at all. It takes a certain mind set to be able to carry out those acts. They must have cold blood pumping through their veins and frozen hearts. How a human being can beat or immerse an animal in a boiling vat or blowtorch them alive and feel nothing is just insanity to me. Looking into the eyes of my other Thai dogs rescued from the dog meat trade is inspiration to push for change – and inspiration to do more for others. If only they could talk, tell me of their ordeals, of how they were snatched and thrown on board like they were nothing but money makers. Who did they belong to? What was their fate to be? I would never know the answer to so many questions but I could still make a difference, and this one, this little miracle had got to me. I was going to do all I could to change his or her life.

CHAPTER 10

The lucky ones

By now, we had quite a few rescues in our pack. In amongst our sled dog team and racing huskies, there were some who had been saved from hideous situations, not just from Thailand but also Romania. As I reflected on what the dog in Bee's photograph had gone through, I thought that one thing was for sure, my girl Coco was likely to have been grabbed by the tail and launched into a cage heading for the same fate, as was Bliss. To this day it's the one area you need to give a wide berth – *don't touch my tail!* she almost shouts at you. She is one of the sweetest dogs ever but has the voice of a warrior when she needs to. And I don't blame her – they think she'd been stolen from her home and was among 700–800 dogs abandoned on a river bank, but miraculously found by the Thai navy patrol before she fell back into the wrong hands.

I'm sure Coco was a stolen pet, as was Bliss. It saddens me so much to think of her troubled past. Just like Coco, I'd seen Bliss on a social media page and she really got to me. Her eyes were unbelievably sad. She was among two hundred other dogs that had been found on the back of a truck and she had recently given birth while amongst many hungry dogs; she then contracted distemper, a viral disease, and had to fight for her little life. She had a troubled little head on her shoulders for quite some time so the fact she was kept in a clinic with little socialising didn't help. But now, she was one of the happiest dogs you could meet; I'd made that promise when I named her Bliss at the time she was rescued.

What I love about these dogs having come from such dark places, some more than others, is their ability to mingle. They seem to know the drill and pick things up very quickly. They know when they're onto a good thing so it's a combination of being happy but not letting things affect them. In fact, it's been harder raising puppies than integrating or rehabilitating a pack that are mostly street dogs.

And finally there was some good news from abroad too. Miracle – the name had stuck by now, it was destiny – had been rescued by undercover officers working for an organisation called the Soi Dog Foundation, a not-for-profit, registered charity in Thailand. Soi Dog existed to help the homeless, neglected and abused dogs and cats of Thailand; they worked to end the dog meat trade throughout the region, and were always there to respond to animal welfare disasters and emergencies. The Foundation had a hugely successful neutering and spaying campaign which had, so far, dealt with almost 100,000 animals. They can't rehome them all but knowing that the dogs weren't going back on to the streets un-neutered was a huge relief. There was though, still, a niggling feeling that the meat traders were never far away . . .

Our Miracle, as it turned out, actually ended up being moved to a shelter in Northern Thailand, in Nakhon Phanom.

As the weeks went by, I worried about the dog rescued from the truck because now he would have been amongst over 3000 dogs in the shelter – all in the same area and lost. I'd asked if Bitter Brownie could search for him/her – it was obviously a relief to know Miracle was saved from the truck but I worried that the longer he was surrounded by disease, the more chance there was of being affected by it, if not already. How could this poor soul survive? I really was looking for a miracle.

As the weeks painfully dragged by I waited for news. With bated breath, I could only hope Miracle had been found and was safe in a clinic; a breakdown in communications hampered news coming through but I had a gut feeling that he was alive and I've always followed my gut. But weighing up the odds, they weren't good. In amongst thousands, where sickness and distemper were rife, it was a breeding ground for new life and disease. A dog-eat-dog existence where only the toughest and fittest survive – or that's what I thought. I tried to keep hold of my positive thoughts despite jumping back to photos of a dog who looked finished, done with life, but that was somehow still breathing. In what state he could be in now, I just couldn't bear to think; this dog just had to show up.

Bee continued to put up photos of her rescues on her Facebook page but Miracle was now just a dog among many. Many well-wishers and hopefuls around the world would scroll the rescue photo pages just like I did looking for Miracle, looking for the facial scars this dog bore. In those weeks, I'd started raising funds, with people donating from around the world, while another friend started up another fund to receive donations. People had been just as upset as me after those first photos were posted and many tried to help. In the process, I was being contacted about dogs people thought may be Miracle. I knew they weren't the same dog but what were their chances of ever getting out? Getting a shot at life? Pretty much zero to be honest. So I asked the people who followed my quest to find Miracle if they would mind some funds going to the lookalikes. I knew they weren't Miracle but nobody seemed to mind – they said that was a perfect idea, and that day, Bee pulled two dogs from the shelter; Miracle was still lost somewhere in the crowds. At least these two guys were now safe and heading to a vet clinic.

However, the search was still on for Miracle – I couldn't give up hope. Another female dog popped up that I thought may have been Miracle, since we had no idea what sex he was at the time. Again, it was a lookalike but I decided to help her anyway, a girl I called Faith.

By this point, we had rescued Ole Man, a beaten looking boy, Spirit, a white girl, and Faith, an off-white girl – all safe now. From donations, the vet fees were paid for those dogs until I could find adopters somewhere in the world. Then I received some sad news – Spirit hadn't made it, she had died. I was gutted; she was so close to a bright future. I knew I could have found a home for her but she was cheated of all that lay ahead.

By accident, a few months later, I stumbled across a photo that looked awfully like her. A little white female who lo and behold, was Spirit! Alive and living happily at a rescue in Thailand, she had made it after all. It turned out that there had been an error in paperwork that meant two very similar dogs had been mixed up. And, in fact, the rescue centre didn't want to part with her so Spirit still lives there, a Thai girl forever. I was sad that the other poor dog hadn't survived, but I was learning to take the good out of any situation now. And even more positively, Faith and Ole Man were then adopted together and are in Canada.

It was now July 2013, 8 weeks after the first photos of Miracle on the truck were seen. By this time I was starting to think the worst – the inevitable – had happened. That dog could only have gone downhill and couldn't have evaded being seen this long in the shelter, surely? Then one morning I switched on the laptop as I sat with a cup of tea browsing the rescue pages and who was staring right back at me? My heart was racing. The dog I'd asked Bee to search for was right in front of me – Miracle! Once I calmed down to a panic, I noticed the dog had two sponsors, two women known as Mo Ni and Bea Gra, and had been called Lucky. But this was Miracle – I was 100% sure it was the dog hanging from the truck, the dog I'd fundraised for and worried sick about for weeks on end. These kind women were going to pay for the dog's vet care and try to find a family to adopt him. So as soon as I could I had to get in touch with them and let them know my efforts to date in trying to track this dog down. After discussions, we decided I would take care of all Miracle's needs.

At this very point, life not only changed for this dog, but for mine and another little miracle in my life. Change nobody would ever have imagined.

I was going to bring Miracle home.

Miracle now has his own link on the Soi Dog page to educate the public. He's a fabulous ambassador against the dog meat trade. They've attempted to give him a back story, I think more to highlight the sick trade that he escaped from, imagining a mother and possible siblings; was his meat laced with drugs to catch him? Or was he a chained dog in a yard, used for security; was he a treasured pet? The sad truth is, we'll never know where Miracle came from. There is one part of the story that stays with me though:

'... *They took us to a shelter and offloaded the truck. The sore on my neck had become infected, so they cleaned it up then gave me some antibiotics. They cleaned up all the dogs that could be saved. Sadly, many had died.*

Those that survived were fed and introduced to our new home in Thailand. There were many, many dogs there though. I'm one of the really lucky ones – that's why I'm called 'Miracle'.'

Nothing was truer! Miracle was a boy, and a boy who was sure living up to his name. This sick dog with terrible skin and seeping wounds had actually managed, surrounded by all those other dogs, to hold distemper at bay. This was incredible. I was ecstatic and yet still found it hard to comprehend that a dog in such bad shape had managed to fight off that disease – but true to his name, he did.

Now, we had the long road ahead to recovery.

It wouldn't be easy. His immune system was low and his skin was terrible; at one point the vets differed in opinion as to whether he had a skin allergy or suffered from demodex. Demodex is a form of mange. It's not contagious but mothers can pass it on to their young from mites that burrow deep into the skin. It's also hard to get under control and Thai dogs live in a humid climate all year round which isn't great for skin conditions. As you read this you'll squirm, but we actually have demodex mites in our eyelashes. Well, the demodex burrows deep down in the skin and can even miss being detected when taking skin scrapings by a vet due to this. Miracle was under treatment and one minute his skin would improve, then he'd have setbacks. I'd asked my own vet for advice and also my friend Britta who lived in Bangkok and had stepped in to help over there. She made trips to visit Miracle and would take or get hold of specific things I felt could benefit him. She was even able to give him vitamins that I wanted for him to boost his immune system. (Miracle actually stayed with her for the week before his trip to the UK, along with a dog called Shadow who was rescued alongside him and now lives in Germany.)

Given I was now in control of all of Miracle's care and rehabilitation, I asked for him to be on a treatment to attack demodex and, over time, it worked. It was truly amazing to see this skinny broken looking dog transform as the months drifted by. For him, that existence must have been a hard one, and mundane, day in and out for nine months.

I was so excited to receive updates and pictures of this boy gradually gaining weight and the sores diminishing.

'Look, Tobias!' I'd shout, as I sat at the laptop.

'Is it another picture of Miracle, by any chance?' he'd smile.

'Maybe . . .'

'Go on then, let's have a look,' he said, giving in as we both always knew he would.

I told all the dogs that they would soon be getting a temporary kennel mate and told the most important person of all.

'Kyle – meet Miracle,' I said, angling the screen so that he could get a good look. 'You might not be that interested now, but I bet when this one gets here, you'll be great friends!'

Of course, I was just trying to keep all our spirits up – introducing a rescue dog to an existing 'pack' is never easy as it can be a very unpredictable, and potentially volatile, situation and I was clutching at straws hoping they would be great friends, but I still had to try. I had read so many stories of children bonding amazingly. Sometimes, especially for those with problems like Kyle's, they even started speaking, finally communicating with the world, or they showed affection and emotion – I hadn't thought this at the time though, that would be beyond my wildest dreams. Yes, Kyle could communicate with us, and yes, he could show affection to us, but it wasn't a 'simple' case of autism with him; he had so many more challenges.

The main reason for bending over backwards to get Miracle was for Miracle himself. I wanted to change his world, not mine. I wanted to show him that there was love and hope out there, and that he deserved a life full of only good things. That determination I had promised myself I would have after all the hardships we'd had with Kyle was coming to the surface. I knew Miracle had been broken and must have been so close to giving up, but the spirit he had shown was something which spoke volumes to me, and I was going to repay his perseverance a thousand times over.

CHAPTER 11

K9s loved and lost

It was true – I had fallen for Miracle (or 'King Miracle' as he is affectionately known to many) hook, line and sinker.

Many people started to ask if I was adopting him myself, but the plan at that time was to bring him to the UK then decide on a suitable family once I'd assessed what he needed. The plan was never to adopt Miracle but merely to save him from the horrors there, get him healthy and find him the best future I could. Just what he deserved – in fact what they all deserve, each and every one.

But I was growing to love this dog, more and more each day, even though we had never met. Each day I felt more for him and needed to give in to the fact that if he came to stay, he might never leave.

I told myself that if Miracle were to join us and our huge doggy crew on a permanent basis there would be some challenges ahead . . . but this rescue bunch was pretty easy to get along with and would predominantly be his canine family. We knew it wasn't a real concern with Kyle either, after seeing how happy and relaxed he was with our other dogs. The real question was – how would Miracle handle it? After all he'd gone through and the situations he'd been in? I couldn't even imagine how troubled he might be and how unsettling that could be for us all. I just had to hope that fate would step in and lend a hand again. I knew I'd love nothing more than to give this special soul all he needed and more. It was just another aspect of our unconventional life – I was never one to conform to the paths my friends chose and always took the long way round. Born in the year of the dog, the only thing missing on me is a tail!

The time drew closer to Miracle's journey to the UK. I had counted the months, then weeks, now we were down to days. So many around the world had grown to love Miracle and his rags to riches story. How a boy destined for the dinner table now had a bright future waiting for him. The world was cheering him on.

By now, the anticipation of meeting him was huge. He'd make his way from Thailand in the capable hands of a rescuer friend called Niz Khan. She and another friend would travel with another 5 dogs also coming to the UK in search of happiness – Felicity, Lady Bee, Sophie, Peggy and Betsy, all girls. It was like Miracle's harem – well, he was King after all! The group would fly to Amsterdam, rest then take the ferry crossing to the UK. All of these dogs had their passports and had done their quarantine in Thailand, and were good to go. Tobias was able to stay at home with Kyle so I'd planned to fly down to London where a friend, Donna, who does so much for rescue dogs, would pick me up so we could make our way to the ferry port, something I was so grateful for because, if you can believe it, despite being able to drive a sled dog team, I have never learned to drive a car!

As we got closer and saw the ferries the moment had finally arrived. I was actually going to meet the dog I'd loved at a distance and hold him. The question was – would he want me? He'd been through so much trauma in his little life so far, was he really ready for this? Could he deal with the stress of the journey back that still lay ahead, on-board a sleeper train from London to Scotland, the crowds, the noise and with someone he had only just met?

By the time we got inside the port and found arrivals, they'd arrived. And then I saw him. My eyes fixed on this little white dog whose eyes wandered aimlessly in wonder of where the hell he was but he was just going with it. I felt that surge of emotion again, all so familiar when about to meet another life saved. I had to keep a lid on it as I approached him; I was so scared to spook him. But when our eyes connected, that was it! I remember this almost telepathic feeling, like he knew who I was and that he'd be OK. The look he gave me spelled out – 'you're the one, you're my mumma!'

I was trembling, it was like being on a date; there's a connection that makes your heart skip a beat and you're nervous and you stutter and go to jelly. Only this was no man, this was the lifeless soul who had survived against the odds. It brought me back to Odin and a part of me couldn't help thinking he'd come back to me somehow. I know it sounds so cheesy but it really felt like our hearts said 'Hello' – he really had me at 'Hello'! He was a miracle. And 3 April was when his life would really begin.

When a dog from a troubled background joins me I'm armed with my 'just in case' kit which involves carrying a harness for the dog to wear then a safety neckline us sled dog owners are no stranger to, which I attach from the collar to the harness. You just never know what can trigger a dog to attempt escaping. I know if the dog slips his collar, he still can't wriggle his way out because the collar's attached to the harness. Some people might use a slip lead in such a situation – they're almost like a noose, so the dog can't back out – but given how these dogs are caught, they can be very sensitive to having their necks touched and I've seen some situations with slip leads go horribly wrong. I personally think they're a recipe for disaster, resulting in traumatised dogs running around lost in a strange country.

The way Miracle walked by my side, so trusting, I knew the kit was a back-up plan. He even lay on my lap as my friend Donna, who had collected me from the airport to reach Miracle at the ferry, drove us back to London to catch the sleeper.

My next concern was how he'd react in the middle of London's Euston station. But I soon realised that it was all in my head. This was a former street dog, after all, this didn't bother him at all. The only thing I had to be careful of was getting on the train and the gap from platform to train (he wasn't so keen on that).

The sleeper train cabins are small and pretty claustrophobic but Miracle didn't seem to mind. Stepping up on the bed, he seemed quite inquisitive as to how he looked in the mirror – he was definitely my dog! Who was this battle-scarred dog staring back at him moving the same ways he did, he seemed to wonder? He ate and drank then settled on the floor fighting sleep as the carriage rocked him back and forth. Occasionally, as the train changed tracks he was jolted and woke again. I just couldn't take my eyes off him, casting a glance over the scars he still bore that had caused him such pain. This was like watching a baby sleep, when you're scared to take your eyes off them, making sure they're breathing. And in fact, there were many similarities really, as I had done this many times with my son since his premature birth. I'd spent the last few years worrying – I'd worry if I had nothing to worry about.

The tracks changed yet again at 2.30am and something wonderful happened: Miracle got to his feet and very carefully crept up on to my cabin bed. He began by lying beside me then crept onto my chest where he lay for hours, with me terrified to move because I didn't want to disturb him. I knew I was right to trust my gut, after all.

Around 6am, there was a knock at the door with breakfast. This former street dog didn't attempt to steal a thing – or maybe he just didn't fancy what I'd ordered. Then it was time to get myself a bit more presentable. After all the attention Miracle had received around the world, I'd been told that a photographer from the *Daily Mail* would be waiting for us at the train station. As we stepped from the train, I felt my eyes well up. Miracle set foot on Scottish soil on 4/4/14, World Stray Animals Day – how amazing was that, we'd not planned it at all! The true survivor and stray had made it on a very special day for strays around the world.

Once the photoshoot was over Miracle had a chance to stretch his legs a little before it was time to head further North. I was trying to break up the journey for Miracle as much as possible and we were lucky to be able to rely on a wonderful network of supporters to get us back home. Incredibly, the photographer who had met us off the train offered to drive us the next part of our journey to just beyond Edinburgh airport, where we were met by another rescuer friend, Kerry and her little girl (who Miracle was so gentle with) who drove us up to Fort William. There we took the train further north to Inverness where we were met by my lovely friend Joanne, who then drove us back to the house – so many wonderful people!

As Joanne drove us over the rattling bridge to our secluded home, the pack howl of our dogs had started up. They can always sense when you're on the way, long before they can see the car, and the sound, to me, is one that says *home*.

We were met by Tobias – Miracle was more wary with him, but I assumed that men had definitely been more threatening to him in the past. And I could hardly blame him. But in that moment, nothing else mattered. Finally the king had reached his castle!

In those very first days, Miracle stuck to me like glue. He had already become my shadow to the point it resembled the way a duckling hatches and thinks the first thing it sees is its mother. He wouldn't let me out of his sight. And I didn't blame him. It quickly became apparent that Miracle's physical scars may have been healing but the mental scars of Miracle's past were very much present and looked like they may be far more difficult to treat. It was obvious he was scared of men but we also noticed he had a specific dislike of baseball caps, something both Tobias and I wear working in the kennels. Miracle would clear 3–4 feet of furniture just to get away so the best thing for Tobias to do was ignore him. We've had nervous dogs around us before and a method where you walk around dropping tasty treats as you go has good results, normally. With Miracle, his worried mind and memories that haunted him were too strong, he just wouldn't risk even the tastiest of food. A former street dog who wouldn't risk being petted for food – starving dogs would usually do anything for food – but still waters run deep. What had happened before he ended up on the meat truck? Sheer horror, that was evident, he was so very traumatised.

I knew Miracle needed the company of other dogs before these problems manifested into separation anxiety and worse. This is where his canine crew did their job and took him under their wings.

I introduced him to little Scarlett and little Coco first. It was a hit – the trio played all night as I sat crying happy tears. It was beautiful to witness, this former Romanian street dog and a Thai girl headed for the same fate playing with Miracle, and it just made me so happy seeing three little lives without a care, playing and just being dogs. This would be great medicine for Miracle's healing.

Moments like those are all the inspiration I need to carry on saving more lives, being their voice and endeavouring to carry that voice as far and as loud as I can. I'm just determined – I'm nothing special and not amazing, the tears I cry for those animals are not important, the tears they cry for help are. When I see those dogs happy at play, I am thinking of the past, a past stored in a memory box that's triggered open from time to time. I think of their innocent little minds, remembering dark times. That's why I do what I do. The mind is such a powerful tool. It has such a great way of protecting from all the bad things that haunt us.

I've been oblivious to this for a long time, but the happiest times I've ever had have been with animals for as far back as I can remember. I think becoming a mother has made me feel it all the more keenly. And the more troubled an animal is, the more I'm drawn to help. Skin issues, burns, scars all give an insight into just where they've been. Some dark place with nightmares that are even darker make me want to help them even more.

I've got a real soft spot for old, weary dogs. They could tell many tales and sometimes their eyes speak to you, needing no voice. I'd rather offer them a month or two of love, even if their time on earth is dwindling.

Skin issues have always affected me badly, which is probably why I was so drawn to Miracle. The hot humid climate of South East Asia never gives dogs peace, and they suffer on the streets in the baking sun. While some restaurants may throw food to street dogs, others are wicked – often, dogs are a target for throwing boiling oil or water over. This is something I can identify with too. As a little girl, I had an accident where I ended up with skin grafts on my arms. I was lucky; the boiling hot water left my face only with superficial burns. I know this has a lot to do with my own sense of my appearance throughout my childhood too. I have no pictures but I know I resembled something from a horror movie and spent two months in hospital.

What didn't help was that, on the day I was burned, I was wearing a little woollen dress – my dad's instincts were to pull it off me, but a lot of my skin went with it. I was emotionally scarred by it and would go into hysterics if I saw scissors. Wrapping gifts was always a trial as paper and ribbons were cut. My mum could never understand my triggers and it made life difficult.

When she spoke to the consultants they said they'd had to cut the skin as it dangled from my arms. I had skin like ribbon back then and I could still remember the terror when anything jogged that memory.

I don't remember a thing about the accident, just the cartoon characters painted on the walls of the hospital. I tucked those memories away in a box until they were triggered again. I had to have years of skin grafts. I was so sensitive and embarrassed about my scars; I just wanted arms like all the other girls. It took me until my late twenties before I started to feel comfortable in my own skin and recognise that the scars I despised were part of my life journey. The one scar on my face sits in my hairline – a small price to pay really. In fact, I've grown to cherish my scars; the one scar I never want to fade is the one that represents the time when my two boys were fighting for their life and I was fighting to keep them safe. I am so proud of it. I think that is why Miracle really spoke to me. His skin was always a problem – it still is – and I see that as another bond between us.

It was as if Fate was saying, yet again, *here you are Amanda, here's something for you to do. Take this dog, take this precious life, and make something from it. Work your magic – use all of your love and show what can really be done when cruelty doesn't win, when good overcomes evil.*

It was a challenge I would always be up to.

CHAPTER 12

The bond

The longer Miracle was with us, the more I noticed Kyle's interest in him and his interest in Kyle.

The more time Miracle had to settle, the more he blossomed, with only the occasional setback or flashback still very much present. The things which bothered him were sudden movements, and men still tended to make him much more nervous than women. He also showed a lot of anxiety around men who smoked, which was a problem given that Tobias did.

For a time, his skin improved too, and then erupted like I'd never seen before. It was really nasty. It could go from hair loss to lesions in a matter of days. I hadn't realised Miracle needed to take his skin medication every month for up to one year so it caught me off guard and scared the hell out of me when it flared up so badly. So I moved him over to a raw diet for his skin and gave him coconut oil (which he adored), vitamin E (because there isn't a part of the body it doesn't benefit), and salmon oil as it marries so well with the vitamin E as well as turmeric. I did have to gradually work up to those things because I had to analyse what was good for him and what might need to be eliminated. The truth was, he started to stand and wait on his coconut oil from the get go. He absolutely loved the stuff and it was so great for his skin.

He stuck to me like sticky rice – a Thai saying that I found very appropriate. But I noticed he'd walk up and give Kyle the odd lick and acknowledge him but never read too much into it.

One day, after about a month since Miracle had come to stay, I decided it was time to check on all the formalities.

'We need to check if your microchip is registered correctly to me in the UK,' I told him. Miracle had to have his rabies jab and be microchipped over in Thailand, or he'd never have been allowed to travel (all dogs need to be processed in their country of origin). At that point, it wasn't a legal requirement in the UK for dogs to be microchipped (it became law in 2016), but I still made sure all my dogs went through the process, just in case the unthinkable happened and one of them became separated from me. I hated the thought that we might not be reunited, so I ensured that they could all be traced back to me.

I contacted the Kennel Club, as was routine when I registered dogs from abroad and explained about

Miracle's situation, which I knew was a little out of the ordinary. Whilst on the phone, I got chatting to the call handler about my new dog and my other rescue guys. We were talking about Miracle's arrival only weeks prior, how he was from the illegal dog meat trade, how I had so many dogs and not forgetting Kyle too, so we laughed about the full house I had to deal with. She told me that the Kennel Club had campaigned against the dog meat trade and I was so surprised by this information – it had never occurred to me that they would.

'It would be fantastic to include Miracle's story in our blog,' she said.

'That's great,' I told her, letting her know more about the Soi Dog Foundation too and seeing how the two could work together in the future. 'In my opinion, raising awareness is exactly what this trade needs to shame it.'

So, true to their word, Miracle featured on their Kennel Club blog informing many thousands of the story of where he'd been, where he'd come from, and the happiness that now lay ahead.

On that same call, the woman asked if I'd ever seen their Crufts *Friends for Life* competition.

'Yes,' I replied. 'I have seen clips of previous years, they were all such tear-jerking stories too – how in the world do you choose?'

She laughed and agreed they were all worthy but it was all down to a public vote once the shortlist was agreed upon, so out of their hands at that point.

'You should enter,' she encouraged. 'It would be perfect – the award is to recognise the really special bond between an animal and a person, and it sounds as if Kyle and Miracle would be ideal.'

At that point, it was such early days. How did Miracle get on with Kyle? So far so good, but all the dogs sense they need to be good around him. I'd hoped Miracle would fit in with our family, but I was always realistic. I really didn't think the pair fitted the criteria even when it was suggested to me so I kind of dismissed the idea.

But as the weeks passed, I started to change my mind. It was obvious that Kyle was particularly interested in Miracle the more time he was around. I also noticed if health professionals visited Kyle to fit him for equipment, Miracle would lie in between them and the chair. Not that he would have done anything bad, but he was making his presence known; *don't hurt my puppy* was written all over his face. It wasn't something I discouraged. Miracle didn't have a mean bone in his body and Kyle clearly sensed his good soul, while the dog could sense a little boy who couldn't speak either but had so much to convey.

Miracle had a story to tell but with no voice, just like Kyle. Neither could spell out what they wanted to say.

Then I started to notice that Kyle would make sounds, not words, and Miracle would walk up to him. We didn't really know much about autism then, having only recently had the diagnosis but the habits, the sounds, the lights, the lack of eye contact were all part of it. But now, not every time, but some of the time, I'd seen Kyle look into Miracle's face, touching his face, really looking at him. Yet he'd look right past us or anyone else – maybe looking at you fleetingly but very briefly. I found this intriguing.

Miracle would bark on hearing Kyle's taxi come home from school and he'd stand at the door as if welcoming his puppy home. But right from the beginning, he never clambered over Kyle and he was never rough. It was like he knew he was special, always acting like a true gent around him.

It was as if there was a little unspoken language going on here. There was definitely something, a little friendship of some sort gradually getting stronger. Years ago, I'd watched Khandi, our rescue Jack Russell, seek solace in kids. She was so gentle yet had been through hell. Before my eyes, I could see that Miracle saw something in Kyle to trust, to be close to, to watch over, something very similar to that I'd seen in Khandi.

As Miracle's character came to the fore he'd dare to be mischievous, to steal what he could from the kitchen, but no more than any other former street dog. It goes with the territory, until one day they realise that food is plentiful and they don't have to worry about the next morsel or scrap. With some, it never leaves them; the years on the streets have been too many and that mind set is obsessed with food. One of our rescues called Old Mumma Mia couldn't resist flipping open the food bins containing kibble and getting a mouthful just to prove she could.

Miracle was still stealing scraps and joining in the naughty antics but seemed to pick up on when it had all been pushed too far and his intuition stepped in to calm him down. He was a dog that picked up on so much and, despite everything, his tail wagged constantly. He would cast his watchful beady eyes over situations, sizing everything up, taking it all in. Getting to know him over those initial months was such an education and I started to see elements of his personality that reminded me of Odin.

Odin was my soul mate of years gone by who had been such an intuitive little character and those qualities were becoming more noticeable with Miracle, more apparent all the time. I just had this really maternal feeling to protect him. Despite becoming more mischievous, he was still so fragile. I worried about even taking him to the vet for his skin condition to be checked. I also had to get him accustomed to travelling in a crate rather than loose in the car. A crate was something most people would never consider for a dog rescued from one, one he had tried so hard to escape. But the lifestyle shared with sled dogs and race dogs involves travelling and being transported safely in specially designed travel compartments. Having Miracle accept travelling in small spaces he would tolerate would be a huge benefit. It makes a huge difference to a dog being introduced to things they've been scared of in the past, helping them realise those spaces can also be safe places in the right setting. Coming from a dog who'd lost teeth in attempts to escape the dog meat truck, those small steps here in my home were truly fantastic to see. He had literally attempted to bite his way to freedom and yet he was willing to do this through feeling secure and trusting and eventually did of his own accord. Feeling comfortable in a crate was key.

But in actual fact, he would snuggle up to a huge white dog of ours called Harlow, knowing he was safe, wanting to feel secure.

Just one week before Miracle arrived, I had adopted this gigantic white fluffy girl from Romania who I called Harlow, after Jean Harlow. She weighed 30kg at 7 months old and was getting bigger by the day (she's now fully grown, weighing in excess of 50kg). To look at a dog that size, it is easy to forget that they are still puppies.

Harlow was settling into her life here when Miracle arrived and the bond was instantaneous. Scarlett and Coco had been great help on those first nights, but these two were utterly inseparable. *I'd nailed it*, I thought – he had a bond that was set to be a strong one, which took some of the focus off me! Canine company would ease him into life quicker than facing too much human interaction. Neither dogs were used to home life; the noises we all take for granted scared the hell out of them. Kettles, vacuum cleaners, washing machines could kick things off big style, but they tried to be brave together and did make slow progress.

The one thing Miracle needed each night was to sleep beside me. Now, as a rule I've never allowed dogs on the bed so technically I kept this up, even if it was with very loose boundaries. I found myself falling asleep most nights watching films on the sofa and Miracle would sleep right on top of me. Not the best night's sleep, but it would just be a weaning process for a while, I told myself – and he wasn't on the bed, we just so happened to fall asleep every single night on the sofa! He felt safe with me but I needed him to feel safe, full stop. He had to let his guard down and accept other dogs as well as humans; even just a little would give us something to work on. This is where Harlow did a great job just by being her, just by being a dog.

The relationship that developed between Miracle and Harlow really played a huge part in him easing his way gently into Scottish life. She'd only arrived from Romania one week before him so was also at a bit of a loose end. She was a great distraction for him, not that he really let his guard down exactly but he did play with her which was so fantastic to see.

When Harlow had arrived I soon realised the giant bed I'd bought her wasn't big enough so, until I could source another, I doubled over a duvet for her to use as her bed. This ended up being a toy for the mischievous duo. Miracle would lay on it while Harlow – who resembles a Womble – would gently grab the duvet and take Miracle on a magic carpet ride around the house to show him the new sights! She would drag him round on the wooden floors as if it was the most natural activity in the world! It was one of the funniest things I'd ever seen. The pair became joined at the hip and no matter the space in any given situation they would finally sleep together and snuggle.

Miracle's huge girlfriend loved him to bits, that was for sure. They would play fight constantly – he would drag her, or attempt to drag her, around while she could fit his whole head into her mouth if she felt like it! Miracle was loved by all the ladies – to watch all the dogs mix from toy breeds to giant made me so happy. In summer they have their own doggy playground to run around in or laze the days away while they sunbathe, and this was something he really enjoyed. Kyle would sit in his swing watching their antics from the garden – they were quite the bunch!

Over the days, the fun and games between Miracle and Harlow became more and more entertaining to watch. They were still doing their tours round the house on the duvet and as time went on, as play worked its wonders, the weeks drifted by and Miracle slept by Harlow at night. They were fast becoming joined at the hip and he was feeling safe with his big bodyguard. Walking them round the fields that surround the house was like being pulled by a team of sled dogs. Not exactly a leisurely stroll but I've always been used to walking at husky pace anyway. You tend to adopt a walk that looks like you're about to drop backwards as the dogs in front are pulling, leaving you no choice but to dig your heels in so you don't take off.

When I had this pair out together, I had to be prepared. Harlow's breed – the Mioritic Shepherd – is used for herding livestock in the mountains of

Romania, and for warding off wolves and big cats. She clearly is curious and calm around sheep, as if she thinks she is supposed to do something with them – she's just not sure what. Miracle on the other hand just barks at all the big white woolly dogs in the fields!

I felt as if he really was settling in. I didn't mean that in a way that minimised his trauma in any way, but it was important to give this beautiful dog a future rather than only dwell on his past. To see him with the other dogs, especially Harlow, filled my heart with joy. But to see him with Kyle – well, that was something that brought hope, something there had been precious little of for all of us for so long.

In fact, the more settled Miracle became, the more fussy he became too! I made the mistake of buying a different brand of coconut oil once and he turned his nose up at it. Not a problem for the other dogs, who were more than pleased for their share, but Miracle was convinced this brand must contain poison and wouldn't entertain the stuff. Fish was great for his diet and skin but getting him to eat it raw was an issue – *raw mum? You think I want raw mackerel, or any of that other fab stuff the fish delivery leaves that smells amazing? Get it cooked – unless it is smoked salmon or trout, that's OK.* The little tinker! He was hilarious – the ex-street dog who'd have eaten anything to get by had decided he had taste and was confident enough that if he turned his nose up something else would arrive on the menu! That smug look as he danced around the kitchen sniffing the fish aroma as it cooked to his liking! For a moment, it would flash up in my mind, 'don't create a spoilt brat!' something I tried never to do with dogs. But then I'd watch him guzzle food like no one was watching and his tail never stopped wagging. He adores raw meat and bones – so much that he'll even dance for them! How I loved this little guy whose personality was becoming so cheeky, happy and confident.

With all of this going on, the request to apply for Crufts 'Friends for Life' wasn't in the forefront of my mind. However, as I watched my boys, day after day, it was becoming more and more apparent that something amazing was taking place.

'Look, Tobias,' I would whisper, 'Kyle is staring right into Miracle's eyes.'

It was true.

The child who never made eye contact, who was locked in his own little world, would stare at the broken dog and I swear it was as if they were communicating across the divide.

Whenever Kyle would get upset, Miracle would rush to his side, quickly but quietly, so that our boy could be comforted by his presence or by holding onto his fur. I started to notice it more and more.

'There is a bond, isn't there?' I asked Tobias one night.

He nodded his head. 'Yes, I think there really is.'

'What do you think then?' I asked him.

'About what?'

I sighed in exasperation. I had been thinking about it for days so I expected him to read my mind!

'The Crufts competition – should we enter it?'

'If you want to, then of course you should,' he said, 'but remember that it could change everything.'

That's what I wanted. I wanted to change everything. I wanted to change the world. I wanted everyone to know about street dogs, and cruelty, and autism, and children like Kyle. I wanted them to rail at the unfairness of it all and sign petitions and raise money and stop the meat trade and make sure that every child who needed help got that help. I wanted this huge big mish-mash of things to be sorted out in the world – but could it be done? Could it be started at least by that very world knowing about my two wonderful boys?

'I think I do – I think I want to do it,' I said to Tobias. 'I think it's time to kick some ass.'

CHAPTER 13

Friends for life

I did wonder whether it was too soon for Miracle to be thrown into something like 'Friends for Life' but I also thought there was little chance we would be shortlisted for such a prestigious award.

Hell, I said to myself, *it's worth a go!*

Miracle really was settling in though at home and could be such a funny dog at times. He had started to walk on his hind legs and do kangaroo jumps across the kitchen to the fridge asking for his food. It was obvious that he had a playful side and I was amazed that still came out after all he'd been through – it was a real testament to the wonder of animals and how resilient they are.

To watch him blossom made me so happy and was incredibly rewarding to watch. He had come so far already.

In those first few months, Tobias reaching out and extending an arm to offer food was still unacceptable to Miracle. Ignoring him seemed to be the best approach. I called Tobias the chicken man because when a rescue dog joined us he would always win them over by dropping tasty food while he walked around; they would then associate him with good things but it did take a while with our little miracle.

'It'll come,' Tobias would assure me.

'I know – you'll be the best of pals one day, but every time I see him flinch when you extend an arm, or shake when he is trying to work up the courage to take the food from you, gives me a flashback just the way it gives him one too,' I said. 'I already love him so much – the thought of what those bastards did to him keeps coming into my mind. I'll never let that dog down, Tobias, never.'

'I know you won't,' he replied, holding me close as Miracle's past sent dreadful images into my mind. 'You'll never let any of them down.'

So, to help even further, Tobias would lie on the floor holding a bit of food, ignoring Miracle deliberately so as to draw him closer. To begin with, Miracle would clearly be nervous but he would eventually creep up, grab the tasty morsel, and then run – there was obviously still something in his mind that made him think a man might grab him, but, as time went on, he realised that Tobias was a different sort of man and he got bolder. The longer Miracle was with us, the more we could break down his thought patterns of fear, and replace them with reliability, regular food, and love.

As I've said before, when you have a child like Kyle, sometimes your relationship can suffer. Tobias was running a business, a restaurant in Inverness, and that wasn't something that worked round office hours, nor was it stress-free. There was always a problem to deal with, and he was always the one who had to fix things. We lived in a beautiful area, but it was isolated – he couldn't just pop into work in two minutes, and I wasn't surrounded by a network of help for Kyle. We both had difficult day-to-day lives, and, unfortunately – like plenty of other parents in our position – sometimes there just wasn't that much time for 'us'. When I said 'goodbye' to Tobias in the morning, I often wouldn't have a moment to breathe until we were lying in bed saying 'goodnight'. We had been together for such a long time and, although I don't think we took each other for granted, we perhaps didn't always make the time for our marriage that would have helped. There just weren't enough hours in the day.

But, little by little, something was changing.

A little white dog was giving us something new, something to bond over – something to make us remember just how strong we were as a team.

'Did you see that?' I would ask Tobias as Kyle would casually extend his arm and hold Miracle's fur when he went past. He was such a sensory guy, a common trait with autism, but this was definitely new behaviour.

'I did – he's doing that a lot, isn't he?' my husband replied.

'Yes – he loves all the dogs, but this one is really taking his fancy!'

It was true – the stroking of Miracle, the tactile communication between them was very obvious by now.

'Amanda!' shouted Tobias one day while I was in the kitchen. 'Come and see this!'

I rushed through to see Kyle holding onto his dog, making very clear eye contact, pretty much staring into Miracle's clear, sparkling eyes.

'He doesn't do that,' I said, referring to our little boy. 'Tobias – you know he doesn't do that. He hates making eye contact.'

'Not with Miracle he doesn't – he's been sitting like that for ages now.'

It was now impossible to ignore that the bond between boy and dog was something very special indeed – and that it was drawing me and Tobias closer. Every time Kyle chose contact with Miracle, the bond between two desperate parents became a little stronger. We only wanted the best for our son, but it's hard when every day seems to offer no new hope, when doctors and other specialists just want to give bad news, when no one else can see that, actually, this is a wonderful boy. People don't know what to say – so they say nothing and avoid you, or they say the wrong thing.

There is no getting away from the struggles Kyle faces, but I still want for him what any parent wants for their child, what I would have wanted for him if nothing had gone wrong. I want him to be safe. I want him to be loved. I want him to have the best life he possibly can.

I'm not sticking my head in the sand – I know how hard it will be for every single day he is with us, but I will never give up on him. To see him with Miracle, to see him reacting and engaging, offered hope. It was as if Miracle was giving something to Kyle that no one – human or animal – had given him before. He was sparking something in my child, and my child was sparking something in him.

I started to wonder if maybe there was a chance, maybe this 'Friends for Life' award was something they had a shot at after all.

It's been so difficult watching Kyle struggle with life so far – he himself is a little miracle. It felt like each time we dealt with an issue involving his ongoing care and advice from medical teams, we were being hit with something else at every turn. It was even more noticeable as he grew older, trying desperately to convey his thoughts, frustration building and, although Miracle was giving him some respite, it could be very hard for a mummy to watch. Having therapists involved, having them give a professional opinion is all fine and well, but dealing with issues on a daily basis is something very different. There would often be home visits to watch Kyle and ongoing assessments almost weekly. It felt odd to open up my home to strangers and to have them assess me as much as they were assessing my boy – I know we have an unconventional life and there is no denying the fact that many of them judged me for having so many dogs while I had a severely disabled child. I don't think many of them actually opened their minds to what Kyle gained from being part of the pack; they would often speak to me as if I was an idiot, as if I was risking my boy's health and safety by indulging my love of dogs, rather than seeing what a benefit the whole set-up was for our entire family.

It is a sad fact that Kyle can't speak. I desperately hope that one day he will, but, for the moment, it can't happen. To hear him say 'mummy' would be the best thing ever. I know he tries so hard. We watched and listened for months to individual letters being pronounced and then he joined those letters to pronounce his own name. It's not clear to all but we know what he's saying. It was a huge achievement, but sadly it barely registered with many of the professionals.

When we were called in for a meeting one day and given the news that Kyle had been assessed severely autistic, it didn't really come as a great surprise as such, but it still felt like being hit by a train. Even though we'd had our thoughts, our suspicions, hearing it was hard, especially given that Kyle was in the room beside us, blissfully unaware of all being discussed.

Medical teams are dealing with cases but this is our son; he's not a number, he's Kyle. They fill in forms, throw ideas into a mix so complex, then go home to their own home, leaving many questions still unanswered with us having to wait until the next meeting to have it all presented again. It's frustrating to the point we've chosen to deal with so much ourselves – we know our son. And now, someone else knew him too.

CHAPTER 14

Miracle the mystery

By this point, I was so excited about entering the boys for the competition. I knew they had a special bond and it was one which I hoped would only grow stronger, but I also knew there was one major difference in their experiences that I could never get past. While both Miracle and Kyle were locked in their own worlds, at least I knew everything about Kyle from the moment he had been born. In fact, from before that. I had been with him almost every second of his life; with Miracle, I would never know. I could guess, I could put parts together from various rescue sites, I could try to make assumptions from photographs and the stories of others, but he could never tell me. I didn't know where he had come from, how many puppies were in his litter, what age he was, or how he had become the amazing dog he was today.

All of this mystery was symbolised, for me, by a tattoo he had on his ear. A series of numbers and letters, it was something I couldn't quite work out. Usually, these tattoos show that a dog has been spayed or neutered on the streets and put back again by the shelter, but Miracle was an entire male when he was saved and it was the vet clinic who neutered him; he already had the tattoo at that point. We have no idea who did it, or why. The clinic didn't do it. There are sterilisation campaigns that neuter and spay – in Romania, they tag the ear afterwards but if the dogs fight or get injured then the tags get torn off, so, in Thailand, tattooing is preferable. But why Miracle? Soi Dog had no idea either. Was he meant for something else? Something more sinister? What could it be? There are dogs who are farmed for their meat – are they tattooed?

The other thing which still bothered me was his skin condition – it really was horrendous. I was told that his mum was probably a street dog, making it likely he picked it all up within a couple of days of being born. I wondered who his mum was, who his dad was? Were they on that truck? Were they with him? It was so hard to look at him lying beside me on the couch, sleeping so peacefully, without a care in the world, and wanting that for every dog – but knowing that I just couldn't achieve it. Yet.

By now, Miracle was settling in with his canine crew just fine. His passive nature saw him accepted with ease. In fact, I imagine this is the reason he survived among over 3000 dogs in Nakhon Phanom's shelter. The fact that he was weak and a quiet, perceptive little dog obviously served him well and helped him survive. Now he was part of the rescue pack – there were nine of them at that stage, plus our old Kuzak who watched over all that went on. It was so funny to see them all, from Romanian Chihuahuas to Kuzak to Harlow – all sizes available at Amanda's dog parlour!

They were such a bunch of oddballs who just loved life. I know that I'm very vulnerable when I watch them all being so happy – as they play I want to save the world, to rescue more and more. But the problem never goes away, there is always another dog, and as I watched Miracle turn into the most remarkable creature, I couldn't help but ask myself whether I should be doing more for animals like him.

The world needs to know, I told myself. *I just have to keep pushing everyone to do something about cruelty to animals, working to make places adhere to welfare guidelines.* It was what I believed then and what I believe now. The more I read about what was going on around the world, the more disgusted I felt. If spay/neuter programmes were obeyed as they should be in Romania for example, the problem could be solved. If the money was spent on the purpose it was intended for, then over the next few years there would be very few strays on the streets. Too many street dogs are culled and this solves nothing – puppies are still there, and they in turn breed more puppies. The culling is in no way humane. The dog catchers are paid for each dog they take to public shelters – or killing stations as I call them. Where there's money to be made, animals always suffer. They always pay the price.

It's one thing to view photos on social media sites but it's another to actually experience the harsh reality and degree of horror rescuers speak of. So, since it was three years on from rescuing my first Romanian dog, and with everything I had promised myself and my family, I felt it was about time I practised what I preached and flew out there to see what I could do.

After more fundraising and a lot of plans being put in place for Kyle, I travelled over to Holland where I met my friend Rebecca at Schiphol airport and we flew to Bucharest together; we knew it would be tough but nothing could have prepared me.

There we met four other rescuers based in Romania, Carmen, Anna, Lonela and Monica. These women all do amazing things, and I was proud to be part of it. They deal with it day in and day out, and had warned me that I needed to keep my emotions under control. The men who run the shelters thrive on seeing visitors upset and if I cried it would be like giving them a gift.

I can honestly say Romania broke my heart; in fact it would be more apt to say it was torn to shreds. Everywhere I went, there were dogs. Dead on the roads, living under cars, on the lookout for food and on the move all the time, never knowing where the next morsel was coming from. Whilst I was there I barely slept. Listening to the dogs during the night, I could tell that every screech of brakes was likely involving dogs.

When Anna picked us up from the hotel on our first full day, the sun was blazing. She was eager to get me to the car and head straight to our destination but there had been a delay. On her way to meet me, Anna had found a puppy in the middle of a country road. This was a common occurrence there apparently as the poor little things just get dropped out of moving cars as they go by. When Anna opened the door, this tiny brindle girl, no more than 3 weeks old, was there to say 'hello' to me. That was it! I fell in love. As I would many times over! She was in my arms the rest of the day while we went in search of puppy milk and food. She had teeth – strong ones – but she was still a newborn.

We bought her a bottle and milk, and this little bundle was so ravenous that she bit the teat off the bottle and ate that too. I'd never seen such a young puppy behave like this – she was tough, real tough. She'd had to be. It's amazing to watch an animal so determined to survive and fight, to not give up even when the chips are down. I guess we all have to just cope as best we can in life.

We named the puppy Anna (affectionately known as Anna Banana) after the woman who rescued her and who does fabulous work there. That evening, little puppy Anna went into the very capable hands of my friend Carmen. She was so little that her best friend became an injured kitten that Carmen had at home and I'm pleased to say they're both thriving and we're now searching for suitable homes. Just by seeing that little puppy, discarded and considered worthless, I knew I was in the middle of a hellish situation. I quickly realised it was impossible to even scratch the surface of any of this without big time help and media. Anna also introduced me to Faith, a girl I'd named a few weeks before after hearing her sad story. She'd suffered a lot and her ear had been cut, common practice apparently. I just couldn't understand why . . . there didn't seem any reason to any of it.

The next day, I visited Carmen's shelter where she had more than three hundred dogs, dogs who have been there many years, some all their lives, three legged dogs, disabled dogs, dogs with no eyes. It was overwhelming as I recognised faces from years prior to this visit, faces I had seen on websites and in photographs. Yet this was a great place where great work was done. The dogs were happy but they desperately needed adoptive families. Carmen had support from two local people who worked at the rescue, but she was a single parent herself and never stopped working. Watching Carmen do her best, I thought, *I have to help her*. . .

I wished I could take them all home with me, but I was only there to look. I had said to myself that, if there were dogs I had to save, so be it, but they would be for other people, they wouldn't be coming home with me.

Then Monica took us to her rescue in Bucharest and that's where I met him.

They called him Benji.

He had the most soulful eyes which looked as if they had been through so much – which was indeed the case. He'd been tied up while some sick bastard tried to skin him alive. It had been done with such precision, such determination to wreak as much horror as possible, and the scars he now had were horrific. My eyes swept over his body, his thighs with no skin, just raw flesh, as he licked my hand, staring at me with those soulful eyes. He'd known such sorrow.

'Oh my poor darlin',' I said to him, as he nuzzled me. 'This is the fate Miracle was heading for, he was meant to be skinned alive too. What sick mind can come up with such brutal torture?' As he looked at me, I broke all of my promises.

I knew I wanted to adopt this dog, no question – I'd looked into Miracle's eyes and promised to help dogs like him so I made up my mind, he was coming to live with me. On top of that, I had to give him a positive name, to reflect all he had achieved.

'Phoenix,' I told him. 'Phoenix – I'm your new mumma.' I hoped he understood that I would be coming back for him, that this hell would soon all be in the past, but it broke my heart to walk away.

That trip was just horror on top of horror. On our final day in Bucharest came the day I'd been dreading – visiting a kill shelter. We were driven there by Monica's husband and I will never forget it; it was called Bragadiru. A public shelter there is not like a welfare shelter in the UK, have no illusions about that.

As I said, I was warned not to cry as the dog catchers find that so amusing. Until three weeks previously, the shelter we were visiting had been run by prisoners and I was assured that being kind to animals was the last thing on their list. We'd had to make up a reason for visiting and we were questioned so thoroughly before they'd let us in. I think we only finally got let in because Monica's husband was with us, and that was only to make sure we were safe. This was a frosty cold place to walk through on a very hot day but I wore a pair of sunglasses just so they wouldn't see my expression. Eyes are the window to the soul after all and I had so many emotions racing through me in anticipation of what lay ahead. I certainly didn't want them guessing my thoughts.

They took our passports (a dubious sign, if ever you need it) and led us to the kennel blocks. I know I breezed through the first few pens as I was trying to stay composed – trying. We were led round by a wretch of a man – actually, he practically marched us through with a clipboard in hand and a cigarette hanging from his mouth. I noticed he had his trousers rolled up at the bottom to avoid getting dirty. The thing was, I couldn't see any dirt despite the many hundreds of dogs all around me. Then I realised why; to see no mess, no poo, it would be easy to think the kennels are being kept clean, but the real reason is that the dogs are not fed.

As I passed a pen, dogs yelped for attention with one even grabbing my leg through the fence. It was heart-breaking. The begging in their cries finished me.

'I want them all!' I whispered to Rebecca, knowing the man was watching even though he wasn't in earshot. 'I'll pay for all of these to get out – and start a list! I'm taking as many as I can.'

I will never forget those cries until the day I die. These dogs have to witness others being killed in front of them and it leaves a scar. Those souls have seen so much – never tell me that an animal cannot feel until you have seen what I've seen. Euthanasia Romanian style can be anything from beaten to death, poisoning, injected with anti-freeze, or stabbed. It's almost unbelievable to imagine, isn't it? So, when I had this particular dog pleading with me, asking me, begging me to get it out I had to make it happen.

In the last kennel block, I saw a big dog lying on the floor, motionless. As I called her or him it wouldn't lift up its head at all.

'I want that one,' I told the guard.

He laughed.

'Not available,' he said, callously.

As well as Rebecca's, we already had thirteen on our list and he was clearly enjoying my distress, just as I'd been warned.

'I want it,' I said.

He just smiled. 'No.'

(I did end up getting the dog after all; she's now living happily in a home in Scotland. I called her Hope.)

I wished I had a magic wand to save them all.

The skinny man had obviously had enough. 'Final!' he shouted and I thought I would collapse with the intensity of it all. My head was spinning and I couldn't get some images out of my mind. I'd seen a mother with seven puppies, all of them bewildered, with no energy to play, and already knowing not to trust humans. I've never seen puppies with such lifeless eyes. Mum had no milk because she had no food and all she could do was love her young until the day they would all die. Every single one of them looked utterly lost, their eyes had no hope. I wanted them too, but I knew there was a limit – the guard wasn't going to let me have any more and I wondered too whether, by drawing attention to certain dogs that already meant something to me, I was making things worse for them.

Our time was up and we were rushed to the office and sized up while being interrogated. We wanted a total of thirteen dogs and we'd have to go through the paperwork as if it was a normal business transaction, it was surreal.

'Why you want to help?' I was asked. 'What you do?'

I tried to keep my answers very short, not wanting to give him emotional ammunition.

'I will take some of these dogs,' I said. 'I have a list.'

He wasn't really interested in anything I had to say – he just wanted to hear his own voice. He loved to talk and I was happy to let him. Sometimes playing the dumb card has benefits – throw a few smiles into the mix with these men and you can often get what you want. It made me sick but it was worth it to help those dogs. Some people just don't take you too seriously when your appearance is perfume and make-up, and that's fine by me because you can creep up on them and bite them on the ass when they least expect it (or have a dog with very big jaws do it for me!). That was exactly what I wanted to do with this guy who was, to be perfectly honest, the scum of the earth in my eyes.

While we were talking, I could hear a commotion from outside.

'What's going on?' I asked, but everyone was running out of the office. When we all got there, I could see what had caused the uproar. A van load of captured dogs had arrived. Some had escaped outside the gates and others were being brought in via cages balanced precariously on a wheelbarrow. God knows how brutal their capture had been, they all looked shell-shocked. They were wheeled to kennel blocks and as I tried to follow, I was screamed at and it was made clear to me that we were not allowed access.

While talking to the boss I saw his eyes go from normal (or his version of normal) to dog catcher mode. A big hound, a Great Dane type of dog, greying in the muzzle, was doing a relatively fast trot in our direction. He was beautiful, a stunning creature despite the fact that he had obviously had a terrible life. I watched as three of them, including the boss, ran and rugby tackled this dog who put up no fight whatsoever. The way they handled him was so unnecessarily cruel that I wanted to weep. I followed them to see what they planned to do; there was no way that they would suddenly become kind and I could only hope that my presence would make them temper their behaviour.

I hoped in vain.

Horrifically, the dog screamed as its neck skin was grabbed and twisted. The rage inside me was building but in order to secure the thirteen lives on our list, I had to keep my mouth shut.

On realising I'd been watching, the boss changed his tune and tried to sugar coat the situation – but I don't sugar coat, I say it as I see it.

'Please put that dog on my list,' I told him.

'No,' he snapped.

'Please,' I repeated, trying with all my might to stay calm.

'I would be so worried for you,' he smirked. 'He is a bad dog. He would bite you.'

'Don't worry in the slightest,' I told him, charmingly. 'I'm Scottish. I bite harder.'

That day I walked away with the heaviest of hearts and listened to more stories of what happens to shelter dogs. On the journey back to the hotel, I sobbed. Some end up in laboratories, some are used in the most horrible ways, and others are killed on site. All are suffering to a degree that is disgusting and cruel, and all to line the pockets of the unscrupulous that take the grants and subsidies, and never do the work they are meant to do. I couldn't help but start day dreaming about a day when we could make sure these people never harm another creature, to have something like 'Band Aid' but for dogs – but that was in the future; at that moment, I just needed to save a few lives. These souls were in desperate need of kind hands, kind words and the compassion that they had never known. Each one with a heartbeat deserved just that if not for a lifetime, then just for the moments they had left.

When I got back home to Scotland, everything I had witnessed preyed heavily on me. I set about raising funds, organising foster places, doing everything I could (with Carmen) to get the dogs on my list out of there. But, at home, things were happening too. My mysterious Miracle, always so delighted to see me back home again, was getting even closer to my little boy.

Tobias said he'd noticed it when I was away and now we both noticed Kyle watching Miracle even more – but we also saw that Miracle knew when it was happening. He was a very waggy dog anyway, but when he saw Kyle's gaze on him, his tail went into overdrive. It didn't stop for the whole time Kyle watched him. It was amazing that he could actually make it wag anymore; you could say anything to that dog and his tail would continuously wag back and forth, but when Kyle's eyes searched for him, or looked at him with such intensity, our little Miracle managed to find extra wag! Kyle would giggle as the tail went into a fury, and the giggle itself was so infectious that soon we were all laughing. That made Miracle even more excited and the wagging kept on and on!

If Kyle was in his playpen or his walker and Miracle walked past, Kyle would reach out and touch the dog as he continued to walk. He liked it to be on his terms, for him to be the one who initiated contact – to be honest, that's how he was with us too. If he wants to do something, it's fine, but if you are the one who tries to make it happen, he's not always happy. The next day can find the same thing being totally acceptable to him; it is impossible to guess.

Occasionally, Miracle would walk over, just to let Kyle know he was there and he was waiting on a response – or simply just to hang around him. Kyle would reach his hands out and touch Miracle's face – there's nothing so out of the ordinary about that, most people would think but, for us, it was unbelievable. Coupled with the eye contact they kept, it was even more special. We had simply never seen this before, not to this degree. He rarely gave us such contact and, when he did, it was very fleeting indeed. It never lasted; but with Miracle, it was a different story. This, to us, was a breakthrough.

I truly believed that Miracle was seeking something from Kyle as well. Broken spirited dogs often seek solace in children. I felt that Miracle homed in on the fact that Kyle was broken too. All of the pieces of the jigsaw puzzle that we were desperately trying to fit together with our boy were seen by this dog as being out of place and he knew not to force it, just to let it be. He knew something was a little bit broken somewhere – just like him, Miracle was locked in a world where he had so much he could tell if only he had a voice, just like Kyle.

'Where did you come from?' I would ask him. 'What hand of Fate brought you to us, I wonder?' He was our little mystery, our wonder dog and I blessed the day he had ever been sent our way.

CHAPTER 15

Can you keep a secret?

Miracle had been with us well over a few months now and was settling in so well as part of our family. I felt as if he had been with us forever. He still had a long way to go, but he was such a loving dog that I knew we'd get there.

Sometimes Miracle's skin would flare up so he would have to stay in the house rather than run riot with his friends in the playground. So, he got used to Kyle's school routine which led to him barking while standing at the window even before Kyle's taxi entered our drive. He'd let me know that his puppy was about to arrive home. It was lovely and something that I couldn't ignore any longer.

Miracle would bark until Kyle was safe inside then trot around him licking his hand, but he'd never jump up. He was so very good around Kyle in every respect. Kyle would reach out and touch him, and they would have their little routine. Routine is key to the both of them. In fact, the whole kennel would erupt when Kyle's taxi arrived and the Romanian mafia and Thai ninjas would run the length of the playground, welcoming him home. Sometimes I think Kyle's world is a little like *The Jungle Book*!

The Crufts competition was on my mind at times, but I was so busy with other things that it was far from dominating my thoughts. One day, the phone rang just as Kyle had come back from school in his taxi. I was putting the ducks and chickens away, and Miracle was trotting around after me, wagging his tail as always.

'Yes, hello, what is it?' I snapped. I hadn't meant to be rude, I just knew I had one of those lists to get through that would look longer when the day ended and I was too busy for cold-callers.

'Amanda?' said the voice on the other end. 'Are you sitting down?'

It was a representative from the 'Friends for Life' competition and she was giving me the news I had never imagined for a moment.

We were in the final four!

This was unbelievable! I'd had a look online at the entries and stopped looking when the nominations were over sixty so didn't even think that we could win, but the woman at the Kennel Club told me there were well over 200 nominations by then! To be told Kyle and Miracle were in the final – well, my heart just burst with pride for them both. I couldn't tell anyone other than Tobias. It had to be kept quiet for now, well actually until the official press launch in London. God, it was hard not to tell, but I kept to my word and not a soul knew about it. The next few weeks were a blur. They desperately wanted us in London for the press launch, but it wasn't as easy for us as it might be for other people. Taking Kyle anywhere was a huge endeavour, but I wanted both of my boys to be part of this. They had to be.

Due to the fact we have a menagerie here, and the work commitments of Tobias, I decided to book the sleeper train down to London with Kyle and Miracle on my own. You're probably thinking I must be mad but it was the only way logistically possible and safe so we could all sleep and were locked in for the night. However, if you've used the sleeper service you'll know that space is very limited. I had been assured that I had a cabin with wheelchair access. Great! I assumed Kyle would have plenty of room as in his wheelchair pram, which isn't as wide as a wheelchair but reclines so he can lay out like a bed, and I had every confidence in Miracle not getting cabin fever. He and I had used this service from London on the day we met and I only had good memories of it. He was super then and coped with the heat in the cabin better than me. So, I told myself that a hot, cramped cabin with a rescue dog and a child with huge additional needs would be easy as pie – and I almost believed it . . . until the day came. To my horror, when we got onto the train and were shown to the cabin, it was tiny.

Once Tobias had got us on board and left, I panicked a little. We had been assured that there was plenty of room and disabled access, but it was nowhere near what we needed. Tobias was right though – there was nothing I could do about it now. We would just have to put up with it for eight hours or so. I knew Miracle would cope but what about Kyle?

We left from Edinburgh on a service that is fifty years old, handrails in places that only hinder, with not much room. There was nowhere for Kyle's disabled pram to recline fully but I made sure he was securely strapped in the hope he'd drift off to sleep. He did but it would have been impossible for me to get it to lie back properly if he had needed it. Right next to the sliding door was a panel of illuminated buttons – any kid would be interested in those, but an autistic child is drawn to anything that lights up and makes noise. I was terrified, thinking, *what if he presses the unlock button and Miracle gets out*? So I made sure that the dog's harness was looped round a pole so that if Kyle did touch the door, there was no way Miracle could escape. I knew it was highly unlikely that Miracle would ever leave my side, but I still couldn't take that risk.

Kyle did sleep – in fact, I had to wake him when we neared London. I'd only slept a couple of hours as I was scared I would wake up when we were almost there and it would be a mad rush to get everything ready. Miracle had slept well as he knew Kyle had dozed off and was safe; we had been nose to tail on the bunk but I was the only one who was stressed really!

I had spent all night worrying about how the day would go. I was on my own with the boys to protect in a busy, frantic capital city, worrying about taxis and getting to the Kennel Club for the meeting on time, and a million other things.

Luckily, I had booked Disabled Assistance and someone did meet us at the other end. They placed ramps at the doorway but they'd brought a motorised cart thinking that Kyle could just sit on it; it proved a little more difficult when they realised he was in a disabled buggy and we were left weaving in and out of the commuter crowds. Miracle did brilliantly – his real street dog spirit came out and he was like a little bullet.

Was I mad taking all this on? Some people would say that for sure. Sometimes, I think that too. There are those who won't take a healthy toddler on a one hour trip as they get too worried, but I just knew this had to be done, no matter what. I could have made it easier on myself and done a trip to King's Cross from Edinburgh in four and a half hours. But what if I'd nodded off or there had been a delay? There is so little space in a normal cabin and so many people who don't understand. No, this might seem the hard way, but actually, it was more practical on a lot of levels. I always think ahead, I always plan. I just had to focus on the press launch and in order to get to that, I just went through the logistics.

I'm a worrier. I worry if I have nothing to worry about. I'm not superwoman – but if I can do things, anyone can. I don't enjoy having to put myself through these stressful situations, I'm fully aware of how many things could go wrong, but I always try to look at what the end result will be. I just manage. I get by. I don't have any magical coping mechanisms. I don't have anything that grounds me when I feel panicky, but I do fear that I might. I've had panic attacks before and I hope to God I never have another (anyone who has had one will surely feel the same), so I just have to get my head down and get on with things. None of us know what is around the corner so it's best to just concentrate on the task in hand and do your best. When there are others dependent on you, I think it's a bit easier. I'm not sure I could do anything just for myself, but my boys need me, my boys need what I try to do for them.

If I looked back on the last seven years of my life, I would never have thought I could have got through. A train journey is nothing. I try to be pragmatic – get on the train Amanda, get the boys settled, get to London, get to the waiting room, get to the Kennel Club . . . take it one step at a time but never lose sight of the bigger picture.

I don't say it lightly when I say I have OCD tendencies, and this plays another part in my potential for finding a situation stressful. Too many people say that they are 'borderline' OCD, when all they mean is that they like their kitchen worktops clear or their knickers folded! OCD is a clinical condition with a specific diagnosis, and it can make life hell. When I check into a hotel, or a cabin, I have to rearrange everything.

I know now that mine is linked to Kyle. *If he is sick and has projectile vomit,* I always wonder, *where would it go? What would it hit? What do I need to move and how could it be dealt with best?* I take it too far, but the what-ifs and maybes do play a big part in my life. In general, I really feel that the dogs and rescue and everything else I do, keeps me sane. A lot of people think I am ridiculous for doing so much, but I've always been like that. Should I change who I am because I have a child with additional needs? Should I fall into line and become some acceptable type of carer due to Kyle's challenges? No. No, I should not – and I would not be his true mother if I did change who I am. He needs someone who fights and who thinks she can do ridiculous things, because we never know when that attitude will save his life. Life's too short – I want to juggle everything. Even though life is hard for a lot of people and there are plenty of us out there doing everything we can.

So, we were in London safely, in Euston station, with no projectile vomit and no dramas! We had a while before heading to the Kennel Club given that we had arrived around 6.30am so we'd been taken to a waiting area for disabled service users, which was perfect, but our peace was soon shattered. I kept hearing a guy saying, 'sorry, this isn't a waiting room,' as people were continually trying to come in, ignoring the obvious signage. After we had been there for ten minutes or so, a large family of about ten people decided to just set up camp. They were noisy and frantic – they were also of

Asian origin, I was pretty certain they were Thai. They plonked themselves beside me and refused to leave, despite being told it was not a general waiting room.

Of all the nationalities who could have walked in *why?* I asked myself. Very quickly, Miracle started acting differently. He had been lying in his usual position that people laugh at – he crosses his paws wherever he is, next to Kyle. The Thai kids were jumping around Miracle, trying to pat him, but I could tell he was unhappy. They were running up and touching him then running away, squealing all the time. I looked at the oldest man in the group, possibly the granddad, whose eyes were just focussed watching Miracle so intently. My protective instincts kicked in and my hackles went up. I thought, *you have no idea what this dog has been through and you probably recognise something in him.* I know their culture is very different and we see dogs very differently, but Miracle was safe now and I didn't want any setbacks when we'd got so far.

There are a lot of Thai dogs who have that specific look; many are very like Miracle. Was he thinking, *my grandkids are running round, I hope that dog doesn't go for them,* or was it something else? It was almost as if I could read his mind. I really felt that he was ready to come in and beat the hell out of my dog if it went further.

I put my hand up to the mum and made a signal to suggest she stop the kids running around. They were so high-pitched, talking quickly and high-pitched in Thai and it was clearly a trigger because Miracle stood up and was not relaxed anymore. Lots of people had been coming in and out since we'd been there but this was different. He hadn't moved a muscle beforehand, but now he was next to Kyle, on alert. In truth, he couldn't fight his way out of a paper bag but in his head he was thinking that he needed to protect us and believed that he was doing that by standing so close to us. His pupils were dilated and his fur was on end. The whole scenario really irked him, he was just so nervous. In fact, neither of my boys were comfortable; Miracle stayed quiet but his posture changed, and I felt that Kyle was picking up on things. The accent and tone definitely sparked something Miracle was worried about, it was really upsetting to see, and there wasn't a damn thing I could do. It was as if he was back in Thailand – it was primal.

They kept coming in and out, the kids kept running in and out, the doors kept opening and closing, but I knew it wasn't that which bothered him – it was the tone of the voices. He recognised something.

Eventually, someone came in for us and we got taken to the taxi which had been organised for us. The cab driver was such a nice guy, it was a welcome change, and we had a great chat about dogs and where Miracle was from.

'Obviously you're from Scotland,' he said in a broad Cockney accent. 'What are you doing going around London at this time of the morning with this pair?'

I just had to say I was down to do a bit of TV work, as I still couldn't tell anyone precisely why I had come down from Scotland with my son and dog. The amazing secret had to be kept until later that day.

This guy loved dogs, had his own, and he was disgusted to learn of the dog meat trade. Everyone always is; it's shocking how little is known about it. When we got to the Kennel Club, the driver wouldn't take a fare.

'This one's on me, darlin'' he said.

What a great guy he was – and I was grateful to know we had another person on our side, now aware of this disreputable trade.

Everyone at the Kennel Club was amazing but I'll admit I was a bit overwhelmed to be there. I remember walking in and seeing all the paintings on the wall, and thinking of the history. I've dealt with these people for years with paperwork for the huskies, but being there was something else. So much history surrounded me and I now felt that my boys were part of that.

The woman in reception, Sue, recognised Miracle straight away which was lovely – she got very emotional when she saw him.

'You have no idea how many tears I've cried over this dog,' she wept.

She bent down and made a fuss of him, while Miracle just wagged his tail and took it all in his stride. Then she took me through and I met the other finalists with their dogs – we obviously had our story but when I heard everyone else's, I thought *oh my!* Hearing the other stories made me realise how important their stories were too, reminding me again just how incredible our bond with these beautiful animals can be.

The one story that stuck with me and touched me most was that of Katy and Folly. She had cerebral palsy but still held down a job and even drove a car – and why shouldn't she? Folly could assist her wonderfully in all areas of life and I was privileged to see her in action, such as jumping up and pressing buttons for the lift as Katy couldn't extend her arm out. They tugged at my heartstrings most, maybe because Kyle has cerebral palsy and it was a life I once dreamed he'd be able to achieve himself, maybe just because they were lovely.

Kyle had been cooped up a lot and strapped in for quite some time by now, so I did feel sorry for him. Kyle doesn't really mind noise or stuff like that, he takes everything as it is and just goes with the flow, but he can get upset if his own personal space is being encroached on too much. I don't tell him what we're going to do as he wouldn't know what I meant, I just let him enjoy the moments that we have. He clearly understands a great deal but we always try to minimise any potentially stressful situations for him. You just have to see how and whether Kyle is going to accept something. If he is happy, he makes happy sounds. In one interview we did when we were there, you can hear him make his squealing dolphin noise which means he is happy. If Kyle wants your attention and is at the other end of the room, he will squeal and if you do it back, it's like a conversation. People must wonder what on earth we're doing if walking around a supermarket – suddenly, he'll go *Ka!* And I'll go *Ka!* back to him. They must think we have a weird sort of Star Trek language but it's just us. The speech and language therapist surprised us by saying this was exactly the right thing to do because naturally children that are autistic like role-play and copying back and forth. Kyle definitely has his own language, it's just that others can't necessarily understand it. He has a happy clicky sound that developed recently – if he's crawling around with a toy and we're watching TV, he sometimes stops for a moment as if thinking what he's going to get up to and I'll hear the whispery clicky noise, and without thinking I'll repeat it and he'll do a squeaky happy noise. Even though he's locked in his own world he still has this interaction with us. He can show happiness, sadness, joy and naughtiness, he knows how to play you – he can still push the boundaries, but the problem is that he can't tell you when he is in pain.

On that day, as everyone made such a fuss of both Kyle and Miracle, I remembered all the battles we'd fought. Most people are lovely to my little boy, but they have no idea what he faces. Not only can he not verbalise what pain or heartache he feels, but when he does try to find a way to make us understand, it is heart-breaking too. Kyle self-harms. He deliberately bangs his head off things, slaps his own face, bites, scratches punches himself, acts out and up in so many ways, just to try and make us comprehend what the world is like for him. But we never will, not really.

The sad thing is that he can't say, 'Mummy, I have a sore tummy'. If he's done something naughty and you take something off him that he isn't allowed to have, he'll hit himself as if he is saying 'bad Kyle'; he knows he has done something wrong. We've asked for help in handling that. If he is sore, the awful thing is that his very high pain threshold because of all he has gone through in the past, makes me think it has to be really awful if he is acting out. He's like a little pin cushion – when the sun shines on his skin you can see all these white marks where the needles and cannulas have been in his veins everywhere. If one of us shut our finger in something, we'd yell – Kyle goes silent. That is so hard. He's a very sensory wee boy, but there are certain things we have been told about the self-harming that suggest that hitting himself is a chemical reaction, there is something he gains, a stimulant, from that. Inflicting pain on himself releases an endorphin they think that helps.

Some people throw themselves into talking to me more so they don't have to think about Kyle – I don't mind, as before I had kids, if someone put a baby in my arms, I didn't know what to do. I know I've said this a lot, but I really didn't see myself as a maternal person, I didn't feel the clock ticking. If someone was offensive I'd react, but most are OK. Understandably and luckily, the people at the Kennel Club and the other finalists were absolutely great; they were interested in hearing our story but had kids themselves so were really nice. I was talking to them all, but also very aware of Kyle's needs and reactions.

His temperature was one thing that bothered me. If Kyle is too hot, he reacts – and he did have a reaction that day. He can't say, 'Mummy, I'm cold', so I probably wrap him up more than I should. He had on a little denim jacket with fleece arms all wrapped up and cosy underneath but that clearly made him too hot when we were doing interviews inside. He started to slap himself and I knew I needed to do something.

I was stood talking to someone about what would happen the rest of the day, when Kyle started to get upset. Within seconds, my son had reached up and grabbed my hair, literally ripping it out by the roots. Everyone in the room saw it and it brought tears to my eyes. One photographer saw it too and asked if he could help; he could clearly see the pain in my face and had a human reaction to it.

'It's fine,' I said, my eyes full of tears. 'He'll be OK if I take him outside to cool down.'

As soon as the cold air hit him, he was fine. But when I came back in it was obviously a concern, so it was decided that the best thing for Kyle would be to do the press launch there and then, for his benefit. They obviously knew what they were looking for with pictures as the shots got underway but I could tell early on that wasn't going to work with my boy. Like I've said before, you can't tell Kyle what to do – he won't do it; he doesn't understand, so you have to go with it and see what works at the time.

On top of that, Miracle is a very gentle dog and doesn't jump all over Kyle; it's just not in his nature to be leaping up on the pram but that's what the photographers wanted. We did eventually get it but they had to Photoshop me out of the picture! I tapped the pram for Miracle to jump up, but even that was something that he wasn't used to doing. It was as if he was saying, 'why do you want me to jump on Kyle? I don't do that!'

Though it was completely ordinary dog behaviour, it was completely abnormal for him.

'If there is something specific you want,' I told them, 'I'll do all I can to get it for you, but you can't just tell Kyle or Miracle to do things – they don't work that way.'

I was like a fish out of water with my mind fixed on keeping the boys safe, but everyone was great in catering for our needs and making us feel as if we were in safe hands. I just kept reminding myself why we were doing this, and how lucky we were to be a part of it. I even felt a bit like Patsy in *Absolutely Fabulous*! Click click click, darling, flash flash flash! It was like being back in my old modelling days, a bit of a break from reality! I wasn't sure which lens to look at and when, but Kyle was so happy at being outdoors that all the problems seemed insignificant. My little Prince Charming. Miracle was also my little hero as per usual – he was on his best behaviour taking on a role he'd never known and striking poses for the paps! The photographers seemed to get the shots they were looking for, so, job done, it was back to the Kennel Club.

When we arrived, we were all treated to the first viewings of our videos – lots of tissues were passed around at that point. It was so emotional to see how important and special it was to be able to fight for what was close to the hearts of everyone, but, for me it was twofold. If it had just been Miracle, it would have been an amazing story, but I had Kyle too. I tried to wind down a little but it was difficult to do as we were surrounded by people congratulating us and wanting to talk to Miracle. I couldn't quite believe it was happening. He was a real little celebrity now.

'You need to get used to this,' I told him. 'They'll all be asking for your autograph next.'

I swear he smiles at me sometimes, and I'm sure I saw a big grin cross his face after that! The truth, however, was that I had more than Miracle to deal with. Kyle has to be looked out for all the time. He had enjoyed part of the event, but he had also been stressed at times. Though I'd had a bit of fun, Kyle was my absolute priority and I had to try and find some balance between all of the people trying to get my attention, hoping for a cuddle with Miracle, and being Kyle's mummy. In the middle of it all, someone said, 'Channel 5 wants an interview.' I assumed they meant with everyone up for the 'Friends for Life' award, but it quickly became apparent that it was just me and my boys who were required. Despite what you might think, the truth is I hate doing anything public. In terms of rescue work, it's just a means to an end for me for the bigger cause, so a wave of panic flooded through me at the thought of national television.

'Can we just get it over and done with as quickly as possible?' I asked the press relations officer.

'Well . . . the thing is,' she told me, 'they need you there. It can't be done in our offices; you need to get across London to the Channel 5 team.'

Aaargh! This was getting bigger and bigger – and I was completely unprepared. Kyle was getting very sleepy by this point, he'd had lots of fresh air and excitement and I very much doubted that he would stay awake for much longer. He dozed on and off as we headed to Channel 5, but by the time we were in the Green Room, where interviewees are held before they go live, he was snoring quite happily. In fact, I think all three of us would have had a snooze given half the chance – not quite the high-living celebrities they were used to, I'll bet!

'Let's not wake him up,' the presenter said, kindly. 'I've got kids myself and my rule is to never wake them if you can get away with it! It'll be a recipe for disaster if we try, so let's just go outside and get it sorted.'

Everyone was so accommodating. I left Kyle with one of the researchers, and strict instructions to come for me if he did wake, and took Miracle outside. He is normally so quiet and he'll do exactly what you ask, whether that is to sit or jump up or whatever, but he was very vocal during that interview. He wanted to tell everyone about the dog meat trade himself, I think. My nerves were settled quickly as they were all so nice to us, and even Miracle's whining – which was just to make his presence known – wasn't unsettling. I was glad when it was over though, and we could make our way back to the Kennel Club. Kyle had slept through it all but woke when we got there. I took a few minutes to take Miracle to the park to stretch his legs (he'd not peed for the whole journey down!), but, really, I wanted to take everything in just as much as see to his needs.

The great folk at the Kennel Club yet again stepped in and looked after Kyle so we could slip out to Green Park (after all, there was something quite fitting about taking King Miracle for a posh pee in the Queen's gardens!). We'd been stuck in a stuffy TV studio so it was so good to get some fresh air, to feel the late winter chill. And it was then that I could breathe a sigh of relief that the day had gone as well as could be expected. Yes, we still had the journey home but the craziest part of the day was over.

I found a quiet spot and took a deep breath when it was just the two of us. He did a quick pee – after a struggle to choose the right place – but refused to do anything else. In fact, believe it or not, he waited until he got home to his own garden! That's how dependable he is; he's a great dog.

But I was in no rush to get back and be thrown into the middle of all the socialising and attention again.

'What do you make of all this, boy?' I asked him, completely oblivious to anyone who might have wondered about the crazy lady talking to her dog. Miracle cocked his head to the side, listening as he always did. 'It's all happened so fast – so much of it. Do you think it'll work? Do you think we can really make a difference?'

I suddenly felt very tired. It had all been mad since we arrived and now I was realising just how big a battle we had ahead of us. Of course it would be wonderful if Miracle could become some sort of figurehead for badly treated and abused dogs across the world, but we had our limits. This trip had shown that we could achieve a lot, and that there were some wonderful people out there who wanted to help, but it was exhausting, there was no doubt about that.

'Well, standing here feeling sorry for myself won't change anything, will it?' Miracle started getting a little more excited, knowing that we were about to move off again and, no doubt desperate to get back to Kyle. 'I can't waste time on being tired, I can't waste energy on stuff that doesn't matter, can I little guy? Onwards and upwards – let's go and see what else we can do! Let's go and get your puppy.'

We went back to the Kennel Club, back to all that history with all the old pictures on the walls, and I felt that we could take on the next stage. Kyle was properly awake by then, so I got him changed and let him have a really good crawl about now that everything for the press shoot had been cleared away. Kyle had his little pull-along dog toy with him that always brings happiness, and Miracle just sat beside him, happily guarding his puppy and watching to make sure that all was well.

Tobias's brother Euan lives down in London and he'd come into town to meet us for dinner. So after a happy reunion with Kyle, we all set off to get something to eat.

'I don't normally have to find somewhere that's dog-friendly!' he said.

'Well, you do now,' I told him. 'Everything has to be dog-friendly when you have such an amazing member of the family!'

My only worry that evening, as we caught up on news and family, was that I thought people might find our story too barbaric and not touch it. But to be in the final four was incredible. I was exhausted – but I knew that the battle was only just beginning.

We were getting the sleeper train back again late that evening, so Euan kindly drove us to the station where we found a little terrace that was perfect. Once we'd got sorted and said our goodbyes, off we went to the waiting area again. I'd already booked assistance, just like the last time, but, unfortunately, it was far from perfect. When you have a child with special needs, you become very aware of the gap between what there is in theory and what there is in practice. Often parents like me and Tobias, and the hundreds of thousands of others out there, are told that there is so much help available, that all we have to do is ask . . . but even when you ask, the dregs you are given can often make it worse. I'm not argumentative just to be argumentative, but I will fight for what I think is right; unfortunately, you have to fight every single day when you have a disabled child. Maybe I'd been in a little bubble with our Crufts trip as everyone had been so helpful, but I had a rude awakening as soon as I tried to get the train home.

The porter who was meant to be helping us clearly hated his job and was having a bad night. He drove up to us in a motorised cart and indicated that Kyle was to get on.

'He can't get on that!' I told him. 'The buggy is far too big – it just won't fit.'

Without even acknowledging me, the porter got off the cart and grabbed Kyle's buggy out of my hands, walking away at top speed.

'Come back!' I shouted, grabbing our luggage, holding onto Miracle, as I rushed after him. 'Come back here, you can't just run off with him!' He completely ignored me as I tried to throw my bag onto my back and pull the case along, while winding Miracle's lead around my hand. I knew he was going to be very unhappy with Kyle being taken away from him like that. I'm sure he could hear the distress in my voice too, which was getting more obvious by the second as the porter was weaving through the crowds so quickly that I was often losing sight of Kyle. I'm quite tall, and I had heels on, but trying to peer over the heads of other travellers and negotiate my way through with my hands full was awful. I was upset, Miracle was upset, and, soon, Kyle would be too.

I couldn't keep up, and I'm a brisk walker.

But I wasn't the problem.

Someone had taken Kyle from Miracle.

He was getting very worried, his puppy had disappeared into the crowds and my wonderful dog couldn't find him. He was peeking through legs one minute, craning his neck the next – but he couldn't see him, he couldn't see Kyle. He started to pull like mad. The route to the train was downhill and it was slippery, so I was convinced that I was going to be pulled over very soon. When we finally got to the train, the porter was there, completely unrepentant and oblivious to the distress he had caused. Miracle was just so happy to see Kyle again, but the porter hadn't learned a thing.

'It's this carriage,' he snapped. 'Get on.'

With that, he tipped Kyle's pram back as if it would be no bother at all to just wheel it onto the carriage – the wrong carriage!

'Will you just stop and listen?' I stated, my voice sounding much calmer than I felt. 'My son is severely disabled – he can't just be manhandled like that; and that carriage isn't even the right one for us. Can you get ramps now please?'

We needed to be at the end of a carriage where the toilets were as that would provide turning room. It wasn't ideal to have to listen to doors opening and closing all night, but I knew from previous experience that we had to be in one of those areas.

He stared at me as if I was talking another language and continued trying to tip Kyle's buggy back. This was intolerable and Miracle was getting more and more distressed too.

I'd really lost it by now.

'*Stop!*' I shouted.

All of a sudden I heard a very broad Scottish accent say, 'First night on the job is it mate?'

'What?' snapped 'our' porter.

'Is it your first night on the job? Because you're certainly acting as if it is.'

It was so lovely, the relief flooded through me and I immediately felt closer to my own home, to our little sanctuary.

The man snapped his fingers and pointed up towards another carriage.

'Along here,' he said to the first porter who was just staring at him. 'Actually, on second thoughts, give the wee lad to me and you go do something else.'

I couldn't even look at the porter who had been so unhelpful. All of a sudden, I just felt so very, very tired. Miracle had almost pulled me off my feet with worry about Kyle, and I just wanted to get home. We had such a long way to go, but with the new porter, I felt we were getting there. He got some ramps, found the correct carriage, and settled us all without any fuss.

Kyle was upset by it all too. It had been a very busy day for him, and it was close to 2am by the time he finally gave in to sleep. The trip North was pretty tiring, although doable, but I was emotionally drained. Miracle felt asleep immediately, which was one thing!

I had booked the train to Edinburgh so that I could get off with him for a little while to do the toilet, and then travel in the first class lounge for the rest of the way. All I could think of was a couple of hot chocolates as a sugar hit to keep me going! We were getting off the train by lunchtime, and it felt as if we had been away for years.

When we arrived at the station, I just fell into Tobias's arms and he knew it had all been a struggle. He knows me better than anyone and would never think for a minute that I would put Kyle or Miracle into a situation they were unhappy with, but I think he felt the sheer exhaustion in me. We stood there, with Miracle guarding Kyle, for a few minutes and then headed home.

Tobias knows when to keep quiet, but I chatted for the whole car trip, getting it all out of my system.

'I'm so proud of you,' he told me. 'I'm so proud of the three of you.'

'Actually, I'm quite proud of the three of us today as well,' I admitted.

Life is always busy at home. There's rarely a quiet moment, but as soon as the dogs hear the car coming – long before any human ear would know what was going on – they set up the pack howl. It's music to my ears and I was happier than ever to hear it that afternoon. It might be busy, it might be noisy, but it's home – and, boy, was I delighted to be back.

CHAPTER 16

Crufts

Crufts is an incredible institution – it is the biggest dog event in the world, and has been around since the Victorian era. Initially set up by Charles Cruft in 1891, it is one of those amazing brands that is recognised by everyone, not just dog lovers. Mr Cruft wasn't someone who had spent all of his life thinking of how to magically come up with a show that would celebrate dogs – in fact, his family had a jewellery business, but he didn't want to become part of that so got a job selling 'cakes' for dogs throughout Europe once he left college. His involvement with a terrier club in London gave him the idea of Crufts and appealed to his showman instinct.

It was launched at the Royal Agricultural Hall in Islington with over two thousand entries. By 1936, more than 10,000 entries were recorded. Sadly, Mr Cruft died in 1938, but his wife took over the show until 1948 when the Kennel Club became the organisers. At this point, the event was moved to Olympia, where 84 breeds were presented, almost double the initial number – these days, it is well over 200! Crufts has stood the test of time remarkably well and is a testament to the British love for dogs – proceedings have only ever been stopped for WW1, WW2, and an electricians' strike in 1954 when workmen refused to disconnect the stands from the previous show that had taken place in the venue.

In 1991, the show moved to the NEC at Birmingham, which is where all my visits had been, and the event got even bigger. By this point, new categories were being introduced to attract even more attendees and TV viewers, with 2004 seeing the introduction of the 'Hero Dog' section with dogs being recognised for bravery, support and companionship. That is now the 'Friends for Life' competition, which was the one that meant so much to us.

There is something very special about Crufts. I know that it has been criticised in the past for encouraging bad attitudes about dog 'perfection' but I believe the overall ethos is one which really supports good breeders and owners. When I used to visit with our sled dogs, I was always blown away by the combination of professionalism and friendliness that I encountered and now, with Miracle and Kyle on board, I was again overwhelmed by how kind people were to us. The Kennel Club's attention to detail and care was pure gold.

Because I had a dog I had to use a different exit to those without, so I had to go through two halls to get out and then arrange a meeting point with the others outside, because Kyle had to be taken another route. It was a real roundabout way of doing things, but designed to help organise the thousands of dogs attending the event and to prevent theft of the dogs. Passes for dogs are imperative. I started to panic when I knew as it was just my worst nightmare. *How can we do this*, I wondered? *How can I take Miracle through so many people, people that are everywhere, it's just so busy*? They were constantly coming through the doors. I thought, I just have to do this, I have no choice. I kept Miracle on quite a tight lead. His ears were back, constantly listening to me speaking to him. He was so well recognised by now too. We barely walked lift without being asked for selfies, people crying and telling me they'd voted for us. I was just telling him he was a good lad, a clever lad, reassurance constantly; then I noticed something amazing. The crowds were parting to let him through. They were actually making way for this amazing, majestic dog of mine. He didn't look the slightest bit nervous at all. He started weaving in and out, looking for the easiest route and taking me with him. It was like the Red Sea parting, the crowds were just opening up and letting him go through.

I have realised a few times now that if Miracle is not in an enclosed space with too many people around or men, he will be fine. He definitely can still sometimes have issues with men, but I will work on that. As I've said, Tobias had a hard time when he first came as

Miracle hates baseball caps and they can set him off (and occasionally still do now), but I've noticed if it is crowded but it is open air or there are escape routes, he is really good. He goes back into street dog mode; he can always find a way out.

I realised I was wrapping him up in cotton wool; I was just being too protective. I was thinking he wouldn't like that, he wouldn't want to do that, but I was wrong. I thought, *Christ Amanda, you train dogs in a certain way to get the best out of them, and you've missed so much with this one.* I've always said to other people, if you want to get the best out of a dog, think like a dog, don't approach it from a human perspective, think how a dog might react to a certain thing, so I just let the lead go loose and took my own advice. Miracle took me through the crowds as if it was the most natural thing in the world. He was absolutely brilliant.

Before we'd left, my friend Kaye had said, 'just keep your emotions aside and remember what you are trying to raise awareness of and keep that in mind the whole time.'

That hit me pretty much all day. I'd pass people in the corridor and the foyer and they would all say, 'is that the Friends for Life dog? Is that Miracle? Oh, this must be Kyle, Oh my God!' Tobias had said, 'hold it together pal', but I was so emotional. This was vitally important for raising awareness for so many causes – indeed, for the fact that we were trying to also raise awareness for something we are still learning about. The autism. We knew Kyle had cerebral palsy but the autistic side was something I had kept at bay thinking, *please don't let there be another condition that we will have to add to the list as he has been through enough.* Life was only going to get harder for him, why did he deserve to have something else hit him like a hammer? That is what I wanted to raise awareness of and that is why I chose to donate any winnings to the Autism Society (and also split with Soi Dog) and not cerebral palsy or an animal rescue. The fact is people know that in China and Asian countries animals are eaten, they eat dog in India and Sri Lanka, though they can still be dismissive. They often say, as if it is funny, 'they like a bit of cat and dog over there'. Well, it isn't funny at all. It got to the point where even I got annoyed when a guy spoke to me while I was at Crufts.

'That's an unusual dog,' he said, as we were coming out of a restaurant. 'What a good looking wee guy. Are you showing him at Crufts?'

'Kind of,' I answered.

He looked at me questioningly, and I elaborated, 'he's in a competition but not showing.'

From out of nowhere, he said, 'well, I like a bit of dog with a bit of gravy!'

'You better watch out or you'll end up in a pot with a bit of gravy!' I snapped. I just can't stand that jokey approach to it all – when you feel so passionate about something, and you know just what those animals have endured, it's all-consuming. I want to give every dog the life I have given Miracle; I want to create millions of miracles so that other people can take animals into their lives; like I've said before, if I can do it, anyone can do it. If you want something, you can achieve anything.

People say, saving one dog won't change anything – but it will. You can change that one dog's life. That's my answer and it always will be, and I get asked a lot. You are never going to eradicate it or stop it in the shanty towns but you can save countless lives, and if you can stop that pain for as many as possible, you have done a good thing. You have changed their life.

My friend Rebecca had come with us for the event and she was fabulous with Kyle. While we were in the hospitality suite, she spent ages walking up and down with him in the pram, sometimes for up to an hour for a time as I spoke to the officials and everyone around me. Later she told me that Miracle never took his eyes off Kyle. When I came back and quickly nipped to the toilet, he never took his eyes off the toilet door. It's not that he whines or looks distressed, he's just very, very aware, very attuned to us. He picks up on everything. Dogs are incredible like that – they know when a child is close to coming home from school or if you're two minutes late with dinner. They don't need clocks or watches; they're just in tune with everything in a very natural way. Our dogs all recognise the noise of the engine on Tobias's car long before I know he's nearly home.

When little Coco first joined us, and she was in the garden late at night going to the loo, she would be fixated if car lights shone and immediately start barking. We know that her shipment of dogs was dumped in the woods, eight hundred of them, packed into cages just like Miracle, left when the drivers fled. They were all sitting on the banks ready to be taken across to Vietnam but the Navy patrol boats found them in time. Was she grabbed at night? Was she hurled by her tail into a cage? We certainly can't touch her there and she is definitely remembering something when she sees lights at night – they are all so very aware of everything. In fact, I forgot one night and lifted a stick to throw for her to chase and she just threw herself to the ground! Sometimes not knowing their history is torture. I know two were pets, the pretty little girls. I know Miracle was a street dog but that's about it. I know our Toby was 3 months old when he was caught and he had to drag himself up at that age, fight for his life. He has issues – he only has five teeth, he can't take anyone on, but in his head he thinks he's very tough. He never lashes out, but I can see his past very clearly. I was thinking of all of them while I was there and Miracle's behaviour made me remember just why I was doing this – if I could raise awareness, then maybe I could help more dogs just like him. If the world knows what is going on, surely it can't continue forever?

Some people say I should be proud of myself for having rescued so many, but it isn't enough. There will always be another one. I can't rest, I can't stop. My voice isn't loud enough so I needed to speak to people who could take it further; if this was going to help, then I would do all I could.

In the past, if Soi Dog showed pictures, I would often see people commenting that they would boycott the countries where these things were happening, but often it was pointed out that the tourism and trade would help the dogs. You can get some good from it, but it is the government that needs to take action. I know this is a strong image but would it be the same if they were a truckload of people, over a thousand, some who have travelled for days without food and water, with crushed limbs? Let them see that the world is watching – dump these poor dogs in front of the Thai government ministers with the world's cameras trained on them and see what they do. Social media has done so much, there are people signing up every day to help these animals, but there is masses to be done. In the middle of all of this at Crufts, as I was shaking with nerves, I had to hold onto that, hold onto the real reason for doing it.

Meeting all the finalists for Friends for Life again was great. Meeting their fabulous dogs who all had amazing stories was special too. Everyone here really was a winner. Kyle got pretty fed up being in his pram and I knew he'd love a good crawl about the floor but there were too many sandwiches and cakes and drinks that would have been tugged off the table. I thought I was avoiding trouble by keeping him where he was but, just as someone came to tell us it was our turn to head to the stage for the award ceremony, I soon realised something else was going on.

'Rebecca,' I whispered, 'Kyle's filled his nappy, there's such a whiff! But we need to get on stage!' I thought he had a tummy upset anyway.

'You're all dressed up,' she told me. 'Don't you dare touch him! I'll tell you what to do – let's go to the other end of the room, give Miracle to one of the officials, but let him stay nearby so he knows Kyle is fine. You hold his arms and I'll deal with the business end!' So we did just that while Rebecca did indeed deal with business. As soon as we were done we quickly got Kyle ready and went to leave. Suddenly, a woman came up to me and said, 'Amanda, what do you drink?'

'G&T,' I told her. 'Why?'

'Because you need a double,' she said, 'you've got fear written all over you!' It must have been clear to see that my nerves were really starting to hit, and Kyle's mishap couldn't have come at a worse time! Tobias had said not to drink, but I knew I needed one or my knees would start knocking. Just after she passed it to me, another woman came over and hugged me. She didn't say who she was, she just squeezed me very tightly and said, 'I want you to know that what you have done is amazing. You have thousands behind you – soon it will be millions.'

'Oh God, don't tell me that,' I thought, 'I'm trying to keep a lid on my emotions.'

'I can't even think what he has been through,' she said, looking at Miracle, as she slipped me her card. I didn't look at it.

My hands were shaking and it was starting to get to me. I knocked back the G&T then we went down. Someone was taking YouTube footage and I was just trying very hard not to fall.

This was it.

All of the finalists traipsed down.

'Follow the spotlight,' someone told me but there were no spotlights! Rebecca was behind me, pushing

Kyle, and I had Miracle by my side. Kyle was entranced by all the glittering lights on the massive 'Crufts' sign at the side of the walkway, and I could hear his happy noises as I walked. Miracle was happy too – probably because he could pick up on Kyle's gurgling – and I breathed a sigh of relief when the spotlights did finally appear. We stood in our place, all four little teams, all hoping that they would be the one.

I was thinking about all the dogs in my past who I had taken to Crufts, who I had walked round those rings with. It was really emotional. They say that a dog never leaves you, it always leaves an imprint on your heart. It was hard, but I think there were some extra paws beside me that evening.

The lights were sparkling and CRUFTS was spelled out in the middle of it all. I looked at Kyle and he was mesmerised.

'Do you see it all, my darlin'?' I asked. 'Isn't it wonderful?' He was so excited, so drawn to all the sparkle and shine. 'Look! Look at the lights!'

I counted the spotlights until I was stood where I knew I needed to be. I have always hated public speaking – I had been told to look above and over people but there were so many attendees there that I couldn't avoid looking directly at someone when my time came, I knew that. My knees were knocking and I felt ill, then from the side of me I could hear Kyle start to groan. He was starting to get a bit narked. Although he had enjoyed the sparkling lights as we walked in, he doesn't like being in direct bright light and was getting frustrated.

'We need to move him slightly,' I told Rebecca. 'Don't worry, Kyle, we'll just shift you to the side a little so that the lights aren't bothering you.' I was concentrating on that and then I realised we had another problem . . . Miracle, who holds it in on the train, who never pees, never poops, who never does anything he shouldn't, must have thought, 'oh this seems as good a time as any'! But he's not like a normal dog who cocks his leg when he widdles, oh no, he crouches forwards, and that was just what he was up to! It seemed as if it went on forever. Under my breath, I was urging him to hurry up, but then I realised that if he started to circle, we were really in trouble! If he circles, he's going to do something much worse than wee!

Thankfully, he didn't and I was able to relax – in fact, I wondered if he had picked up on the fact that I was so nervous. Had he done it to distract me? It made me stop wondering about Freya, Kuzak, Matz, Odin and all the other dogs whose ghosts were haunting Crufts for me that day – he was just incredible. For me, to have a street dog there in the place where they had been was so emotional. To have Miracle represent not just dogs like him, but *my* dogs too was hard and emotional. Him doing what he did made me forget, it took the heartache away and then I was brought back to the moment.

The videos of all the contenders were played on a huge screen. When they spoke to me, I was tongue-tied and spoke absolute gibberish. Everyone had to tell their individual story then an award was given to the man who had been involved in the Manchester Dogs

Home arson case. He was so touched that he couldn't speak, and I think we all had a tear in our eye. Pen Farthing, a former winner, then came on to present the Friends for Life award. Pen was a soldier who started bringing dogs to the UK for servicemen and women if they had already known each other on deployment. He rescued a dog himself that had been used for fighting and then started up his own charity, Nowzad. I've always wanted to do that, and still do, so meeting him was a real treat. Pen had won in 2009 and was now holding the red envelope containing the name of the winner. It was special for all of us that he was there, and meant a particularly great deal to me because I so admired him and aspired to what he was doing.

As we waited for the results, I looked over at Kyle. He was so happy now. Like many autistic children, he moves his hands around at times as if he is trying to catch the light, making patterns in the air, and that is exactly what he was doing at that moment. He was in his own little world, but very happy there.

I was in my own world too, so much so that it came as quite a shock when I heard the words, 'and this year's *Friends for Life* winners are . . .'

Like an Oscar nominee, I plastered a smile on my face that I knew would stay there no matter what. To be honest, all of the other dogs were so fabulous that I knew they were all worthy but . . . this would mean so much to us; it really could change the world.

But, then they said it. They said the words.

'. . . winners are . . . Miracle and Kyle!'

OH MY GOD!!
We had done it!
We had actually won.

The hall erupted. There was applause, cheering, tears and such a sense of joy. It was such a special moment when Pen came over to us with the award. He bent down to Kyle and held the crystal vase towards him, which Kyle grabbed onto straight away. As Pen tried to carefully prise it away, Miracle jumped onto him just to watch over everything, a gentle reminder that he was looking out for Kyle. They were indeed friends for life.

I couldn't believe we had won. I was speechless.

I gave Kyle a kiss and then bent down to Miracle and hugged him so very tightly. I told them I loved them both and was so proud of what they'd achieved.

'We're going to change things, Miracle – you and me and Kyle . . . we're going to save lives, boys. This is just the start.'

I cry even thinking about it.

It was all a blur of interviews and photographs, and then we were whisked off to do a live TV interview by Clare Balding! The woman who had given me her card earlier reappeared – 'I told you that you had so many people behind you, didn't I?' she said, smiling. Only when I looked at her card later did I see she was a Kennel Club Executive.

Rebecca kept me sane throughout the whole experience, and my boys did me proud. When I got back to the hotel, I peeled off my leather-look leggings and sank into the bed. My high heels had lasted and I hadn't fallen down at any point! I took Miracle's tartan bow tie off and settled us all down for the night. It was over – and it was just beginning.

I stroked Miracle's head as I felt sleep wash over me in the hotel room. This bundle of love and wonder had come so far. On previous occasions I had been at Crufts with other amazing dogs, but they were there to be shown, there to be admired for their lines and their ability. This dog was all about something else. He was about hope. That a little street dog, who had been rescued from the jaws of death, had worked such magic in our lives against all the odds felt like an absolute blessing. To have such a dog represent so many others made me immensely proud. I could hear my boy sleeping soundly. I could hear Miracle's little whimpers that meant dreams were sneaking up on him too. And I felt that this was just the start; this was the beginning of something so big, so filled with love, that nothing would ever be the same again.

This dog would leave his paw prints on the world.

The next day I saw Susan from the Kennel Club.

'You know what you have to do now,' she said, looking me straight in the eye.

'Yes. Yes, I do.' And I did. I had said in every interview that this was a great platform and I was going to make the most of it.

CHAPTER 17

My hero

I spent the next few months doing all I could to raise awareness, just as I had promised. What I didn't know was just how many others were trying too, often from unlikely sources.

Until I was involved in dog rescue, I had no idea just how much the *Mirror* newspapers did to raise awareness of the plight of animals that had been cruelly mistreated. They campaigned constantly and, every year, with the RSPCA, hosted an event called the Animal Hero Awards. This was an amazing night during which lots of people who did incredible work came together with some equally amazing animals, to be recognised for their achievements. There were lots of different categories such as Caring Animal of the Year, Rescue Animal of the Year, and Vet of the Year.

Hold on – Rescue Animal of the Year? I thought when I heard about it. *Miracle, my boy – we're on the march again!*

What I knew now though, was that the time in between entering one of these competitions and actually finding out whether you're on the shortlist, never mind the final decision, can seem like a lifetime. During that time, I started to reflect on just how far Miracle had come and realised that there were two events that had really shown what an incredible dog he was.

A few months after he first came into our lives, I took Miracle to a fun dog show event in Aviemore that my friends had organised. It was held in a huge field and there were all sorts of things going on, to raise funds for various charities. At that point, Miracle's skin was in a terrible way with wet lesions all over, including on the side of his face. However, I decided we should have a day out, so bundled him, Harlow, Coco, Bliss and Bambi into the van. I'd also brought along one of our dogs, Dixie, to represent our working sled dog team.

The woman running the event on the day, Sue, knew that I was a bit self-conscious about Miracle's skin. I didn't want people thinking he was neglected or badly treated.

'Leave it to me,' she said. 'They'll know exactly what is going on by the time I've finished.'

True to her word, she then proceeded to make a tannoy speech to the assembled crowd in which she told them Miracle's story and where he had come from, what he had suffered, and how I was bringing him so much love and care. 'Look at that dog,' she called. 'Look at what Amanda has achieved – now, put your hands in your pockets for Soi Dog and more souls like Miracle can be saved.'

Everyone was in floods of tears and they all wanted to meet him. I was hosting a stall, selling peanut butter and banana cookies I had baked so Sue sent everyone to me. 'Ask her anything,' she said. 'Meet them both, find out how traumatic it's been for that poor dog, then help raise funds!' I sold out in minutes!

Sue, however, wasn't quite finished with me.

'I'm starting them all off on the agility competition next,' she said. 'Why not enter Miracle?'

'He won't do that,' I laughed. 'No way!'

'Why are you laughing?' she asked. 'I bet he'd surprise you – go on, try it. Everyone will get behind you.'

She was right. Miracle was a dream and everyone adored him. He was so trusting, the only thing he wouldn't do was 'sit' but neither would my other two Thai dogs, they both go up on their hind legs too.

There were white markers on the end of planks that had to be negotiated, there were weaving poles, there were jumps and hoops – Miracle did it all. The crowd was in uproar, they had never seen anything quite like it, and neither had I. He wasn't keen when I tried to coax him through a tunnel as it was far too dark and we ditched that quickly, but everything else was a breeze.

At that point something popped into my mind that I went back to as our adventures progressed – *it's as if he's lived before*, I thought. It's like Miracle is a human in a dog's body. He thinks like us, he really does.

What struck me more than anything was the way in which he would do anything for me – combined with the way he was with Kyle made me think that it was almost as if he felt he had to repay us for rescuing him. It wasn't necessary; I would love Miracle no matter what, but what he had brought to the Leask family was really remarkable.

The second really clear memory I have of his amazing strength of character had, again, been apparent not long after he arrived, perhaps about five months into his Scottish life, as I think of it. It must have been September as autumn was starting to get a real hold on the countryside, with the trees turning a beautiful russet colour and the evening sunsets painting a picture every night. We had some friends visiting from Australia and had gone out for a walk with them, by a river, with Miracle and Harlow too. It was still hot, and I was wading in the river with the two dogs to cool them down after they had been chasing each other, great friends as always.

Miracle was looking fantastic. When I first saw him I didn't really know what colour he was as he was so dirty, but now, he was a glorious white, shining in the autumn sunshine. His coat was very similar to that of a short-haired husky and, as he moved, it was as if he was gliding with his toes barely touching the ground.

My friend remarked on how strong his pull was, just like one of our huskies. I soon ate my words! When we got out of the river, Miracle started to pull more and more. He was in a harness and I had to keep walking faster and faster to keep up; then I jogged; then I ran as he upped his game! Everyone was laughing, but I was thinking, my God . . . this dog wants to run!

I kept thinking about how keen he had been, and decided to see what it would be like if I wore proper boots and not the wellies I had on. Had I misjudged how enthusiastic Miracle had seemed just because I couldn't keep my feet terribly well? I took him to the fields, just the two of us, and slipped on a normal walking harness. I would usually use a specific one for the sled dogs – it involves me putting a belt around my waist with a lead like a bungee cord. With that type, there is no shock to the dog's system or to your back when it pulls back and forwards, but this time I opted for the normal one. Miracle adored it immediately.

Canicross, as it's called, is such a good way to bond with your dog, but I had never thought he would be so ready so soon. It's a recognised sport and it is perfect for the way we live, it works all different muscles for the dog and is fantastic training. Canicross is becoming huge – we always start off puppies this way as they are so eager to pull that, as long as you walk briskly, it's perfect (as long as you can keep up with the dog). We may add it to our sled dog business too – it's such a great way for a rescue dog to bond, but also for any dog with a desire to pull. The way Miracle picked it up made me realise that he would do anything I asked of him. He has absolute trust in me, and I am so honoured by that. I'm going to progress from running with him and then attach the lines and harness to a bike or scooter designed for us working as a team together. as he clearly is a dog with a huge desire to pull. I will never put him in a race situation, but, recreationally, he adores it.

As I remembered these occasions, I was struck again by how astounding it was that this little white angel had come into our lives. But the fact was, there were animal angels in many, many lives, and we were in competition yet again.

Our category in the Animal Hero Awards was whittled down to three contenders. As well as Miracle, there was an elephant called Anne and a pony called Twiggy.

Anne had been held captive for more than 50 years, languishing in chains, forced to perform circus tricks. With the help of many wonderful charities and the support of actor Brian Blessed, she had been rescued, and now lived in Longleat surrounded by people who loved her and who would never degrade her again. The footage of Anne was heart-breaking – when she had first been brought to Longleat, she had to be shown how to walk where she wanted, to use her own free will, as the poor creature had been controlled and terrified every moment of her past life.

Poor Twiggy had been abandoned by the side of the road when she was just a tiny newborn foal. She was rescued by the RSPCA and now performed a wonderful role as a therapy animal in care homes and hospices throughout Surrey.

How could we compete? These animals had been through so much too and, although I naturally wanted Miracle to win so that we could continue to raise awareness, I knew that Anne and Twiggy would fly the flag as well.

Tobias and I decided not to take Kyle to the Awards. His paternal granny thankfully offered to come up and look after him, while we had a very rare break together. It wouldn't exactly be a holiday, but it would be a couple of days away from the reality of home and it would mean less strain on Kyle as well as the event would be late in the evening and very crowded.

The preparations began in earnest – by that, I mean that we looked everywhere to get the perfect sparkly collar and bow tie for Miracle! I went down to London a few days before Tobias as I had set up some meetings with businesses and groups who were inspired by Miracle's story and his journey, and who I hoped would help our campaign – like I said, things really were motoring since Miracle appeared on Crufts and we were getting so much amazing support.

The Awards people had booked us into a swanky hotel complete with doorman, and I couldn't quite believe that we were getting such wonderful treatment. All of our meetings went better than I could ever have dared to hope, and by the time Tobias arrived, I already felt that we were winners.

Some of the other people and animals who were up for awards were also staying at the hotel. It was lovely to hear their stories too. One of the dogs was a delicate little whippet called Holly who had been rescued from a puppy farm. She had only known cruelty, forced to deliver litter after litter, until she found a home with a lovely young woman called Amy. What Holly didn't know when she first fell in love with the emaciated, toothless dog was that they would form a remarkable bond, with Holly able to sense whenever Amy was about to fall into a potentially fatal diabetic coma. When Amy's blood sugar levels became dangerously low as she slept and she suffered hypoglycaemic attacks, Holly would race for help. Before Holly came along, Amy's mum would get up in the middle of the night to check her daughter's blood sugar levels, but she now relied on the dog's amazing talent and the whole family could rest more easily.

There was also a beautiful black dog called Pepper who had originally lived in Crete. When her owner, Georgia had been on holiday, she was threatened by a group of men. Pepper, who was a street dog, had saved Georgia from attack by barking and snarling at the men until they left. When Georgia got home, she couldn't get the dog out of her mind. She made up her mind to go back to Crete and see if there was any way she could find her saviour. Amazingly, Pepper was still on the same beach at the same spot! Georgia brought her back to the UK but was in for another surprise when Pepper gave birth to six puppies soon after; all of them now live with Georgia's family and friends, and the story was an incredibly heart-warming one.

There was also a police dog called Stella, a Staffie who had been living as a stray when she was taken on board by Gloucestershire Police. They trained the dog who was now an expert in sniffing out all sorts of contraband from drugs to guns, with hauls of up to £25,000 at a time.

What amazing dogs! We chatted to each other a fair bit as we waited for the Awards to take place but I was so nervous. People were telling me that they had heard things, that Miracle was definitely going to win, but I didn't believe it. The others in his category were amazing, and, as always, I thought that they all deserved it more. Pepper and Stella and Holly were in different categories to Miracle – I think I would have fainted with nerves if I'd had to face Anne the elephant or Twiggy the horse at breakfast!

As we waited for the limo to take us to the event, it was clear that everyone was nervous. Our dogs meant so much to us and we all had campaigns to promote; the level of awareness that could be gained from winning such an award was huge, but everyone wished each other well.

'I don't know how I'll get through this,' I whispered to Tobias. 'I really want him to win because it could be an amazing platform, but is there really any chance?'

'I think there is,' he told me. 'I really think there is.'

I was wearing a tartan dress and heels that I could barely walk in, while Miracle had a black tux collar and a glittery silver bow tie.

'Aren't you handsome?' I said to him as we waited for the car.

'Aren't you both amazing?' said Tobias.

After a lot of confusion with the limos, we finally sped off to the hotel where the Awards were being held. All around us were famous faces who had done so much for animals, people like Brian May and Ricky Gervais, celebrities who really went the extra mile. The room itself was huge, with chandeliers covering the ceiling and gilt chairs around perfectly laid tables. There was to be a meal for everyone before the event itself got underway – 'just to jangle my nerves a bit more!' I joked.

Miracle was really well behaved, sitting at the side of my seat, but it was cramped for him and there were so many people constantly going back and forth. Yet again I marvelled at the nature of this amazing dog – how could he bear it, how could he cope with so many strangers pushing past, with the noise and unfamiliar surroundings? He just did – and gave me a whole lot of strength by doing so.

Finally, it was time for the show to start. It was hosted by Amanda Holden and I was delighted that the people I had got to know were doing so well. Holly the whippet won, as did Stella the Staffie, and Pepper the beach dog.

'Are you seeing a pattern here?' someone asked me.

'Yes, they're all incredible' I replied.

'Well, yes ...' they agreed, 'but they were all staying at the same hotel as Miracle. The winner's hotel I think!'

'No! That's just coincidence' I said, but my heart beat a little faster.

Suddenly, it was time.

It was time for 'Rescue Animal of the Year.'

On stage, a short film was played of Miracle, Anne and Twiggy. It's one thing looking at the photos of Miracle when he was rescued and knowing all that he's endured, but they'd actually got footage of his shipment being taken off the huge truck. Seeing the very footage of his truck moving on the night he was rescued is something I struggle to deal with; it makes it all so much more real. I sat with my hand over my mouth, every emotion rushing through me at once, stroking Miracle . . . and praying.

Denise Welch, the much-loved *Coronation Street* actress, was introduced on stage to present the award, and I closed my eyes. Time seemed to be drawn out forever, and yet it was all over in a flash.

'And the winner is . . . . Miracle!'

He'd done it!

He'd done it again!

I felt overwhelmed – but knew I had to get us both up on stage. As we weaved through the tables full of so many recognisable faces, I was just concentrating on my footing and reaching the stage in one piece! As we made our way, so many thoughts were running through my head. Would I make a speech? Could I? Would I be too emotional? Oh my god, what would I say? But before I knew it, Miracle just climbed the stairs like the star he is. Amanda Holden was waiting to greet him with open arms . . . but Mr Miracle just breezed straight past, on his way to collect his award! Amanda simply laughed and said, 'Well, it's the first time I've been mugged off by a dog!' Y'see, Miracle is a one woman man ;)

And no, I didn't end up making a speech. I was very emotional and reckon I'd most definitely have fluffed my words and not got out what I really wanted to say. It just would have come out wrong so, yes, perhaps a missed opportunity but this really is only the beginning . . .!

Standing there, in front of so many people who were heroes to me for the work they do, my own little dog was recognised as a hero too.

Once the applause died down, we were whisked downstairs to the Press room for a round of photographs and interviews. Miracle got lots of pictures taken with everyone, including Denise, who was delightful with him. She had recently lost her own dog and I felt that created a bond. She was so down-to-earth and friendly ('move your arse over here, Miracle!' she told him when he wouldn't strike a pose), that it helped calm my nerves a lot.

As we made our way back to the table, I kept my eyes fixed on Tobias. He looked ready to burst with pride.

'You did it! You did it!' Tobias said, clasping my hand and kissing me.

'He did it!' I reminded him, looking at Miracle laid on the floor beside us. 'Our remarkable, astounding, magnificent bundle of white fluff did all of this . . . all I did was see a photograph, remember.'

'And what a photograph,' he said. 'What a photograph and what a dog.'

The rest of the night passed in a blur. There were more awards for more animals, and for the people who did so much to help them. We were introduced to a bunch of celebrities, had so many people offer to help us, and Miracle took it all in his stride. How could I ever have doubted it?

Tobias had flown down from Inverness for the Awards – there was no real need for both of us to do the long train journey down and it meant Kyle was left without one of us for less time, and we could get a lift back from the train station too – so the next morning he'd booked an early return flight home. I was more than used to travelling with Miracle by now though!

I was very flustered on the initial journey though. The taxi driver had taken me all round the houses to get to the train station and, when I finally got there, I only had ten minutes until departure. I was loaded down with luggage and I had Miracle to deal with. Rushing along the platform, I was getting more hot and bothered by the second, and just wanted to collapse with a cold drink, my dog at my feet and watch the miles fly by.

As soon as I sat down though, I could see a problem. On trains you either get tiny toilet cubicles – not much bigger than the ones on budget airlines – or the massive ones with sliding doors, more like street toilets that you could get four people into ... or certainly one and a dog! There was no way Miracle and I could get into the smaller type together, but that was exactly what this train had. The thought of a cold drink stretched out in front of me, but I knew that Miracle's bladder was much more impressive than mine; he could manage the eight-hour journey no problem, but if I had so much as a drop of water, I'd be in trouble! I'd just have to not think about it and cross my legs until Tobias picked up us. I would never just hand Miracle's lead to someone else and ask them to look after him for a few minutes, so all I could hope was that the train would be quiet and quick!

We had just pulled away from the platform and I had only been sitting down for a few moments with Miracle settled at my feet, when I heard a man's voice say, 'oh dear, oh dear, oh dear!' as he walked towards us.

I looked up and there was a bloke, in his fifties or thereabouts, looking at me and Miracle.

'Hold on,' he said, 'hold on just a minute.'

'Is something wrong?' I asked him.

'You've got a dog,' he exclaimed, stating the obvious.

'I certainly have,' I replied.

'Well then . . . we've got a problem,' he went on, shaking his head. 'You see . . . I've got a dog!' With that, he gestured towards a very fluffy, very overweight Shih-Tzu at his side. 'We're on the train as well! You've got a dog, I've got a dog . . .'

He looked bewildered and there was nothing more he could say; he'd run out of all the obvious statements!

'It'll be fine,' I told him. His dog looked perfectly placid, and while I'd hoped for a uneventful trip, his broad London accent made me think he would only be on the train for one stop, so I could go back to just reflecting on my trip as soon as he left. 'My dog won't bother yours at all.'

'Teddy's a good lad,' he told me, squeezing into his seat and plonking him on his lap. 'Mind you, I'm going all the way to Berwick – it's a long way for a dog!'

It was indeed – and there went my hope that he'd only be there for one stop! As the journey went on, we got to talking about our dogs. The man lived in Essex but he was taking Teddy to his son's home; he openly admitted that he and his wife hadn't the time for Teddy any longer and that the poor little dog wasn't even getting walked. At his son's house, there would be room for him to run about, and he'd hopefully lose all of the excess weight he'd piled on. Although I was horrified to hear him openly admit to all of this, he was obviously upset and I was glad that he was being responsible enough to take action which would, hopefully, make the poor dog's life better. Too often, people just get rid of dogs they no longer see as part of their lives, and the consequences for the animals can be horrendous.

Miracle really wasn't bothered by Teddy at all. The man was fascinated by his story though, and we chatted for ages. 'Look at those eyes,' he said. 'That's one clever dog you've got there.'

I couldn't agree more. We'd achieved so much on our trip away, and now that home was getting closer every minute, I felt so energised. By the time we got to Inverness, I was desperate to follow up on everything that had happened – even more desperate for the loo though! The lack of a toilet stop for eight hours hadn't bothered Miracle at all – despite Teddy and him enjoying bowls of water together – but I wasn't made of such strong stuff.

'Take him!' I shouted at Tobias as he walked towards me at the train station, and off I ran!

I was desperate to see my little boy, but, when I got back from the Animal Hero Awards, nothing could have prepared me for how he was. Covered in bruises, Kyle had obviously been self-harming more than ever before. Often, if he gets too warm or too worked up, it triggers his self-injurious behaviour. Taking him outside can help so his gran had been wheeling him around outside since six that morning, desperately trying to distract him from whatever was causing him to take out some inner pain on his own body. It's so difficult – we're never sure exactly why he does it, though we've become more aware how the scratching, biting and hitting out can be a result of something else that has upset him. In the past, I'd even convinced myself that Kyle didn't want to come home from school because of his meltdowns. Now we know these traits and Kyle's triggers, and Miracle helps too. But it was still incredibly hard to see – a mother's guilt is bad at the best of times, and I just had to remind myself that I'd gone away to try and help Kyle, to try and raise awareness for him and Miracle. It wasn't easy.

When Kyle finally settled for the evening, I went online. There were so many wonderful memories from my trip and I was looking forward to catching up with all the media coverage and photos, but one thing was niggling in the back of my mind. A man had spoken to me at an event a while ago and told me that Miracle was a Jindo. Jindos are a breed of hunting dog, known to have originated on Jindo Island in South Korea. They are renowned for their fierce loyalty and brave nature – just like my Miracle. I had sort of dismissed it back then as he was just Miracle to me, but it was preying on my mind – there was so much mystery about this dog who was taking the world by storm. The tattoo, his refusal to die, his complete trust in me – was he a Jindo after all?

I was taken aback as soon as I started my search. On every site there were pictures of dogs who could be Miracle. The white coat, the proud stature, the kind eyes – *was this it*, I wondered? Was I finally putting the pieces of his life together? I'd already considered that he might be a Jindo-mix after a woman at Crufts had made another comment, now I wasn't so sure. However, he was so like the dogs on these sites and the many comments about the nature of Jindos seemed to fit him perfectly.

They are housebroken automatically.

They are super-clean – they have self-cleaning coats, the dirt just falls right off and they are extremely fastidious about the condition of their fur, grooming themselves like cats, as well as having no doggy odour.

They are aloof with strangers – they are incredibly loving with people they know, not just their owners, but a correct Jindo temperament means that they will ignore or avoid attention from strangers.

They are quiet. They don't bark or yap for attention, a socialised Jindo only barks when they feel it to be absolutely necessary.

They are wonderful guard dogs, having a strong sense of territory. They work very hard to maintain borders and protect their families.

They are incredibly intelligent – these dogs were bred to think for themselves; they have very strong problem-solving capabilities.

They are very calm and quiet inside the house – as adults, you hardly notice they are there until they come by to check up on you. They don't even like to go on furniture.

But, as always, Miracle had to be different. When I read on, and saw the list of negative traits in a Jindo, they didn't seem to apply to him at all.

Jindos have very strong pack hierarchy instincts – they can bully other dogs. They are a very dominant breed and do not easily make canine friends after their puppy years.

Those trails could all be attributed to huskies but this is not a trait I recognise in Miracle. He really likes other dogs and I have never seen him act like the huskies, for instance – if they took against another one, they would turn around, pin that dog to the floor, and then stand over them until their dominance was established. The only dog Miracle has ever taken against was one called Bobby, who I fostered for three months before he went to a lovely family. Bobby was full-on and really clingy with me. Miracle didn't like that, but he put up with it for a while until he'd finally had enough. Bobby pushed and pushed and pushed at him, then, one day, Miracle gave him a little nip just to remind him that he was a guest here. He then looked at me, very guiltily, wagged his tail as he came over and sheepishly gazed up into my eyes as if he was saying, 'sorry Mum, but he was just annoying me too much!' It's the one and only time I've ever seen him lose his temper at all, and, even then, it wasn't much. To be honest, I could see where it came from as Bobby was certainly an attention-seeking little devil! But he was a Romanian puppy with a hellish start to life trying to find his way. Perhaps Miracle sensed that too? I'm happy to report he's now an adored pet living a charmed life in the highlands.

They have a strong prey drive. Adult Jindos are not suitable for living with cats or very small dogs, unless raised with them. They just look too much like food.

This isn't Miracle at all! He absolutely loves the small dogs, and never shows any aggression or attacks them whatsoever. In fact, sometimes he even grooms them. It's almost feline, he's very gentle.

This has just served to heighten the mystery of our King Miracle even further!!!

But you know what? Whatever you are, Miracle – you have changed our family forever. We thought we were saving you, but you saved us. It was as if Ty was my first miracle but I had to let him go before another miracle could come into my life. Families who live with a child who has additional needs can be torn apart. They only have so much fight and sometimes, when everything is so hard, you turn on the people who are on your side. You, my darling dog, made us see what matters. We always knew we loved each other, but it took one very special dog to make that clear at a time when things were all becoming too much. I won't stop fighting; I'll fight for Kyle and I'll fight for you, I'll fight for other animals, and I'll fight for justice, but I'll have that extra bit of energy knowing that you are on my side and that you will do anything for our boy.

Tobias

I guess there are some people reading this book who will think I'm a bit of a shadowy figure – that's fine by me. I'm happy to just be the guy who hears that there is another dog needing to be saved, another rescue coming to live with us. I'm more than content to be the one who goes out to work while Amanda does everything she does, and just agree to whatever plan she comes up with next. And the reason for that is that I love her with every part of my soul.

This woman has been a whirlwind since the day I met her. She has more energy, more enthusiasm, and more heart than anyone I've ever met. I've known for such a long time that there is no one I'd rather spend the rest of my life with, but as time has given us more and more challenges to deal with, it has made us stronger. Yes, there have been difficulties. Yes, there have been bumps along the way. But we are a team, and I have nothing but admiration for the woman I am proud to call my wife.

Does she drive me mad? Of course. Does my heart sink every time she shouts, 'Tobias! Come and look at this poor dog!' Without a doubt. She makes me scream and laugh, I get frustrated and I get elated, but I can't imagine ever being with anyone else.

What I want to say to everyone reading this remarkable story is this – my wife doesn't want pity, she wants action. She doesn't want sympathy; she wants an end to cruelty. But, I know what she's doing. I know what this is all about, and maybe, just maybe, some of you will too.

She is trying to fix the world because she can't fix Kyle.

She is trying to mend all of these other broken souls because she can't mend the one that is our little boy.

She has never heard him call her 'Mummy'.

It's that one thing that gets to me.

We lost Ty and that was awful. Carrying that tiny white coffin is something that I'll remember for the rest of my days, but our other baby did live and we have to do what we can for him. Amanda does so much – she laughs with him, talks to him all the time, plays with him, does all of the appointments and assessments, fights his corner every second of every day. And she doesn't get that tiny little thing back. She doesn't get her boy putting his arms around her at the end of the day and saying, 'love you Mummy.' She will never, ever, ever give up on that child. Nor will I, but I am very much aware that she was the one who carried him – who carried them both – for twenty nine weeks, and in those weeks, her fighting spirit was honed. It was agony to see her in such physical pain, and then to be emotionally wrecked at a time when she had to be so strong. I knew she could battle for the world when she needed to, but I just wanted to fix it for her. For all of us.

And she deals with it every day. I go to work, deal with menus and suppliers and staff and customers. It doesn't matter how bad my day is, I know she goes through more. But we're a team, a fighting team, and I will never say no to another dog because if that's what it takes to keep her going, I'll be there every step of the way.

I always used to say we'd have it all – the house in the country, the children, the dogs, the business. The irony is – we do. We got it all. And it's been hell. However, we're still here, we're still fighting. I couldn't have done any of this without her and I'd never want to be without her for a single day.

My wife, the woman I hope to spend the rest of my life with, can move mountains. Ty and Kyle could not have hoped for a better mother. None of the dogs who have been in our lives could have wished for a more wonderful person to have chosen them. And Miracle could never have got this far unless this remarkable individual had happened to click on his photo one day. They will all do so much together. What that street dog has brought to our family is immeasurable. The bond between him and our son is so special and I thank whatever fate has brought him our way. If Kyle gets the slightest bit of comfort in his little life, I am always so grateful, and Miracle has given a lot more than that. I hate that he went through so much in Thailand, but I count my blessings that he ended up with us.

It is heart-breaking to see your child locked in a world from which they have no escape, to have no words, to have no means to express what awful torture they may be experiencing. That Amanda has found the ability to tell his story means the world. If it has touched you, don't let that be the end of it. I will shamelessly ask that whatever has made you cry or smile or engage, sparks something that will make you take it further. Whether it is Kyle's story, Amanda's battles, or Miracle's bravery, please hold that in your heart and do whatever you can – write a letter or run a marathon, sign a petition or give up your job and move to Thailand to save these dogs if you want. It all matters. We all matter. We can all battle this – we can all work miracles.

Finally, I want to take this opportunity to say just how proud I am of our family, of every member, canine and human. We might not fit the shape that is expected of us, but we hold so much love and fight in our battered and bruised little gang that we can take on anything.

I love you Amanda. I love you Kyle.

And Miracle? What can I say? Looks like she was right again, you little star!

THE TAIL END

THANKYOU

Thank you to everyone who has written to me or shown their support – we couldn't have done it without you.

The following beautiful poems were written for me by June Burden, a wonderful woman who has her own struggles to deal with and who was incredibly touched by Miracle's story. I am delighted to include them here and share them with everyone.

Unity

A boy locked in a silent world
reached out his tiny hand,
the dog that no one cared for
seemed to understand.

223

Tenderly he stepped forward
over discarded toys,
knowing what he needed,
this special little boy.

He licked his little fingers
he smelt his tender skin,
and all at once a laughter
came from deep within.

The boy turned his head around
and showed an interest, so far rare.
In a world of silence and confusion
this dog had entered there.

He knew this boy moved differently
from the boys he'd seen before,
so carefully he reached into his lap
and laid his faithful paw.

Both these souls had seen so much
both journeys fraught with pain,
it's almost as if these angels sent to Earth
are reunited once again.

© June Burden
March 2015

Miracle

Thrown about on this truck
down many winding roads,
On a one way trip to hell
I've been told.

Hot, cramped,
some of us die,
I don't think we'll see
another blue sky.

The cries of despair
in my ears do rain,
apparently we taste better
if we suffer more pain.

If only man would come
to realise,
there's just loyalty and love
for you in our eyes.

We sense the smell of death
in this old meat truck,
many will lay down,
many have given up.

Some have already crossed over
they just couldn't wait,

I think the old dogs knew
at the market, their impending fate.

I pushed my head through the bars
in a vain last bid to break free,
It was only then that I saw it
a camera pointing at me.

Little did I know you heard my prayers.
An angel came that day,
He paid the seller for my worth
from hell we walked away.

The photo went across the world,
people saw my plight,
many thought my life was worth
putting up a fight.

Now my name is Miracle
Scotland is my home.
Please help 'meat dogs' just like me
find a miracle of their own.

© June Burden
2014

The Journey

The big white dog lay at her feet
far away from a world that saw him as meat,
look a little closer, his scars are still there
testament to the horrors he once had to bear.

They prayed for a miracle that you'd survive
when hanging from a truck, barely alive,
your progress was slow, thank God you pulled
   through
to be an ambassador for others like you.

The white dog lay his head in his paws
until startled by the loud applause,
following his Mistress, his head held high
the audience clapped as they passed by.

Above the stage on the big, bright screen
were pictures of a horrific scene,
the white dog hanging from the dog meat
   truck
battered and torn with eyes tight shut.

Once more the white dog, sat at his saviour's
   feet
now named 'Miracle' his journey was complete,
his Mistress held the award high in the air
saying 'this is for the dogs, still suffering there'.

A well-deserved award, for two new stars
a lady from Scotland and a white dog with
   scars,
as they exit the stage, he pricks up his ears
at the clapping of the audience, wiping away
their tears.

WELL DONE Amanda & Miracle

© June Burden
October 2015

Ask Amanda

There are some questions I'm asked which come up time and time again, so I thought it might be useful to answer a few of them here. Some of these questions are difficult, but I'm not one to shy away from anything, and it is only right that I address any issues people may have about this whole topic. These are just my views, but – as with everything else you've read – what you see is what you get with me, and what I've written here is just my honest reaction when faced with these queries.

What do you say to people who point out that there are lots of dogs in UK shelters? Why bring a dog from Thailand or Romania or elsewhere, when there are so many on our doorstep who need homes?

They're right – there are a lot of dogs in UK shelters, far too many. Dogs that were bought as Christmas presents, or designer-mongrels that were disposed of as carelessly as an old pair of shoes; status breeds, or puppies who grew bigger than expected. There are genuine reasons why some dogs end up there – bereavement or illness – but far too many have their whole world shattered through the selfishness of humans.

However, some rescue centres have such strict policies in place that there are people who *would* adopt from them, but never get the chance. Some don't allow any dog to go to a family with children under ten, but this shouldn't be a blanket policy as every family and every situation is different. Some won't allow dogs to go to homes where there isn't someone there full-time, but there are old dogs who do very little other than sleep all day and who would be perfectly happy alone for a few hours as long as they get toilet access and company when they need it.

I absolutely agree that there should be stringent checks in place but, what worries me, is the lack of flexibility in many cases. That means that there are people who want dogs, but who are prevented from having them due to nothing but bureaucracy. Should we just leave those opportunities behind? Of course not.

If someone is right for a dog, then a dog should be given that home, no matter where they come from. I would love it if there were no dogs in UK shelters, but that will never happen, and I'm not willing to support any argument that says foreign dogs are unwelcome until it does.

The other point I would make is that, for some people, the emotional pull of a dog from abroad is amazingly strong – something in their story makes a connection, and it is a connection that can hit like a bolt from the blue. It's all about personal preference, just like someone who goes to live in a foreign country or marries someone from a different culture. Again, if all checks are done and that person is right for the dog, then bring them together. Happy, safe, loving, *lifetime* homes for all dogs is what I want; I don't care where the dog comes from.

Hopefully by reading this book, it's given you an insight into the harsh reality of cruelty that a lot of animals, not just dogs face abroad. It's something we just don't see here, not on such a large scale anyways. And to know there are governments making money from their 'programmes' for street animals is disgusting. The truth is that, there wouldn't be so much funding available if there were no strays on the streets so the cycle of abuse is perpetuated to increase profits. Remember, the average wage in Romania is only 200–300 euros per month and dog catchers can get 75 euros per dog so where's the incentive? It needs to change!

When you rescue a dog from abroad, aren't you just making a space for another one to take its place?

Again, I can see where this argument is coming from, but I can't close my eyes to the cruelty that goes on. What people need to remember is that, as well as many organisations rescuing dogs, there are also widespread neutering and spaying campaigns running which will, in time, really reduce the number of dogs who roam the streets in Thailand, Romania and other countries (campaigns that are frowned upon, particularly in Romania, for reasons previously mentioned). These dogs are often street dogs, they aren't necessarily bred for meat. Many vets have confirmed, if this is done properly then the number of street dogs will drop significantly as the effect of the programmes kick into place.

Education – and education of children in particular – is so important too, and that is something which is running alongside rescuing and spaying/neutering work; it is my dearest, heartfelt wish that the next generation will see just how wrong it is to treat animals in this way and they will be the ones who finally end such a cruel trade.

When you rescue from abroad, the severity, degree and frequency of cruelty is horrendous. Yes, there are badly treated dogs in the UK too, but when those cases are uncovered, there is usually an uproar – not so in many countries where eating dogs is perfectly acceptable, and where abusing them in the ridiculous belief that this will make the meat taste better is a commonly-held fallacy. You can't change the world overnight, but you can change the life of that dog – you create a future for a life that was hopeless.

Why rescue from abroad when UK shelters are putting healthy dogs to sleep?

For me, as I've said above, it's the degree of cruelty that is simply unbearable. You can give them a future they had no idea would be possible. Seeing the fear of those animals on the streets, how helpless they are, and how precious a mere piece of bread is because they've no idea where the next morsel comes from, really puts things in perspective. There are dogs who are terrified to make eye contact in case you've singled them out for a beating.

A common problem with some of these rescued dogs is that they don't like collars, or to be touched, or pulled on a lead. These things can bring flashbacks of the noose from a dog catcher's pole that strangles, kills, has dogs in excruciating pain that makes them bleed from their mouths as they are being lifted off their legs, their necks bearing their body weight as they are thrown into cages to be taken to kill shelters. When you have witnessed that, I challenge you to say they aren't worth it. They are all so deserving but it really comes down to personal choice; I've adopted from both UK shelters and internationally, and I haven't prioritised one over the other. I've just gone with my heart and I hope that's what you do too. And remember, some dogs will take longer than others. I'm working with severely traumatised dogs at the moment, but just to see a wag of a tail or interaction with another dog, or a lick of your hand makes it all worth it!

How can I help?

This is the best question of all, because it means that the book has really meant something to you, and that you have been touched in some way by our story. The other great thing is that there is so much that can be done. I know that it can sometimes seem very bleak when we constantly hear reports of animals being mistreated, but we have the power to shout; we are their voices, and we should never underestimate the potential for change which can come from that.

Social media is such a wonderful tool and I would urge everyone who has read Miracle's story to go online and read, read, read. Educate yourselves, even through the tears. You will cry, there is no doubt about that – I still do, I'm not hardened by any means – but you can make a difference too. Even if you don't feel you can do anything concrete, pass it on. Tweet, reshare on Facebook, because you never know whether the next person who sees it because you did is the one who will do something amazing.

Fundraising helps enormously – it's key for what I'm setting up myself – and there are many charities who would be delighted if you could have a coffee morning or bake sale for them, even bake some dog cookies! There are so many rescuers doing all they can to fight this very tough fight. Soi Dog Foundation, who played such a big part in Miracle's story, help so many dogs, and I'm particularly close to a registered charity in Romania run by a wonderful woman called Carmen.

I went to Romania to visit her and to see the situation there, and she has been an inspiration to me. If you visit naturedogshelter.wordpress.com, you will be able to find out all about their work, and maybe think about their 'adopt at a distance' scheme. For only ten euros a month, you can adopt a dog who stays there, paying for its food, and perhaps even contributing a little extra. Ten euros goes a long way there and I know that Carmen is one of the good ones.

There is so much that everyone can do from donating what they would spend on Christmas cards, to knitting jumpers for tiny dogs with thin coats who are so vulnerable in the shelters. Sponsored events at your children's school might be an idea, or asking for a dog to be adopted from a distance for your birthday each year would also be a lovely idea.

You have no idea just how you can change a life, give a life a chance and be part of making a difference. Some dogs will be unsuitable for adoption but many are just waiting for their very own miracle!

How easy is it to adopt a dog from abroad and how much does it cost?

If someone has no objection to cost, they can fly the animal direct from Thailand into the UK. However, you pay VAT & tax on top of the flight. Costs vary according to airline, but are usually about £1000. If someone is already going to Thailand to collect a rescue dog, they can add dogs as excess baggage which cuts down on the cost. It's cheaper to fly to Amsterdam and then get a ferry to the UK; this cuts out VAT and tax, but you have to take travel into consideration, such as collection at the port. There are many options, but this allows flight fees to be cut by hundreds of pounds.

All rescuers deal with the necessary requirements in the dog's country of origin. All dogs must travel with passports, and they must all be microchipped, spayed/neutered and vaccinated in order to get them. Romanian dogs are slightly easier to adopt; different regulations in every country mean the process is slightly quicker there. Vets in Romania are much cheaper than the UK too, so costs are lower. When the dog comes to the UK, it's a legal requirement for them to stay in a registered kennel for 48 hours. From there, the new owner arranges collection or liaises with a transport network. Naturally, all potential homes have to be checked too.

A dog from Romania would incur fees/costs of £500 at the absolute maximum in total (including papers, travel, spaying/neutering and vet checks in the UK). The Romanian dogs tend to be those saved from rescues, or the streets, and the Thai dogs are often from meat trade trucks.

No matter the dog, it is vital that you work closely with the rescue shelter so that they can match you to the right dog – and that you only deal with reputable rescues. The last thing these poor animals need is to be given a lifeline that is snatched away from them a short time later. So, please, please don't even think of adopting if you aren't willing to make a commitment to the dog for the rest of its life. Every house move, every addition to the family, every change to your lifestyle all has to incorporate this animal that has been through so much. Don't do it on a whim or to make you feel good for a moment. It is something that needs thought and years of dedication, but is incredibly worthwhile when it works.

If you can't take on a dog full-time, please do consider adopting from a distance by setting up a small monthly payment for one of the dogs in pounds who cannot be rehomed due to traumatisation.

Will you ever feel you have enough dogs?

This might surprise people, but yes! We are lucky that we have the space to take in so many, but there has to be a limit. I have to put my own dogs first and not just keep adding to the crew. It's not about being able to afford that one trip either; you have to have the time and the facilities because things can go wrong. If I can't bring an animal over, I'll do all I can to organise help in other ways, whether through arranging for pallets of food to be delivered or paying foster/sponsor fees. There have been times when it is actually cheaper to bring them over and use my home as a temporary base while I find suitable homes, but this is far from ideal. I am a sucker for a sob story, but there are so many sob stories out there, so many awful tales, that I do have to draw the line somewhere.

What are you going to do next?

I don't feel as if this part of my life is finished! I will always be Kyle's mumma, and I will always fight for my dogs, but I need to spread the word and keep campaigning. My dream is to set up my own charity – 'K9 Miracles' – and to get as many endorsements as possible so that more people know just what is happening. Social media is vital to the global cause. I'm on a mission to meet Noel Fitzpatrick, the Supervet – I have a few dogs that could benefit greatly from his amazing work. I'd also love Victoria Stilwell, the dog behaviourist, to be a part of the cause. I really think that taking her to some of the foreign rescue shelters to assess traumatised dogs would be a wonderful thing, and I would also like her to evaluate the dogs I have at home as some of them are difficult.

On a personal level, I'm hoping to make more trips out to Romania and I hope to make the journey out to Thailand – to the place that has changed my life. I know it will be so emotional, to see the very places Coco, Bliss and Miracle lay, hid and survived. However hard it will be, I know it is so important and will be further inspiration to go on creating more K9 MIRACLES.

I'm also developing a business idea which has been on hold for some time – there just aren't enough hours in the day! I create stunning silver jewellery (it's ironic given Charles Crufts own background in the jewellery business too!) out of your pet's paw prints using their actual DNA to make memories which people can treasure for a lifetime – 'Give me a paw and I'll make you a memory'! And I will definitely do it, with the best canine models of all, I just need to find a bit of time. I've sat on a business plan for 3 years now but one day, one day, very soon!

How can I contact you?

Please feel free to send any letters for me (or Miracle!) to my publisher. I won't be able to get back to everyone, but I can assure you that I will read every single one that is sent. Ebury Press is at: 20 Vauxhall Bridge Road, London, SW1V 2SA.

You can follow me on social media too of course. My accounts are:

Twitter: **@Miracle14332891**

Facebook: **Do You Believe In "Miracles?"**

Acknowledgements

There are so many people to thank, so many people who have been on this journey with us. Writing this book has been therapy for me; though hard at times, it was worth every tear. It has brought back memories I'd buried and tried to forget, yet also raised some I'd long forgotten but which have been very welcome. This journey through life has driven me to exactly where I now know I was destined to be, where I should be. Forging onwards and upwards for Kyle's future, building a business inspired by the dogs I rescued and, very soon, hopefully launching my own charity to help K9 Miracles around the world. Miracles do happen and I, for one, am a believer.

I must thank my husband, Tobias, who wondered in which direction I was heading – I think he now finally realises I stop at nothing when it involves rescuing an animal. It makes such a difference to have support and help, to have him encouraging me and always pushing for me to strive for my hopes, knowing that, one day, my dreams will become reality.

And to my sons Kyle & Ty for teaching me valuable lessons I'll take throughout my life and the public for voting us to win Friends for Life!!!!

There are so many people to thank who've touched my life in some shape or form. The nurses who worked so hard to see Kyle make it and live his life outside of hospital – Janice, Lorna, Vivienne, Margaret and Barbara, thank you for helping us sleep more easily; knowing that you were on shift allowed us to rest, assured that he was in safe hands. You eased the pressure we felt among the turmoil that was our life and I'll never forget what you did. And to Alison for all the tears we shared in the ICU. And to Rob Le Taxi, thank you for being Kyle's buddy and getting him safe to and from school.

To Carmen, for introducing me to my first Romanian rescue and to the street dog crisis dogs face in that country; you inspired me to do what I do today.

To Bitter Brownie, for fighting her fight against the dog meat trade, saving three of my dogs, and for taking the photo that saved Miracle's life.

To the Soi Dog Foundation for bringing me Toby, who had spent six years waiting on adoption. They are now the largest organisation fighting the dog meat and skin trade, and they save animals every day with their hard work and dedication.

To all the independent rescuers around the world making their own impact by saving lives.

For those of you who were part of Miracle's rescue journey – especially to Joanne for that final leg home to our front door – for the support from well-wishers, for the donations to fund his care and trip to his new life, for everything that made it happen.

There are so many people to thank around the world – Bitter Brownie (Bee), Mo Ni, Bea Gra, Dr Kom, Britta, Terri, Niz, Donna, Kerry and Kaye. Also thanks to Rebecca for all you do in rescue, and to Cindy for aiding me in adopting my first Thai dogs and for all the work you and Derek do.

A special thank you to The Kennel Club, The Kennel Club Charitable Trust and to Eukanuba for all their help and support, and for the opportunity to help me raise awareness for such important causes. They also have a great range of food, specially adapted for all our dogs. Miracle's skin is really improving thanks to the help of Eukanuba's 'Veterinary Dermatosis' food and our sled dogs are powered by Eukanuba's 'Performance Food'.

And to my sled dogs who share my life and love of racing – the cold mornings training runs, the sound and rhythm of your breathing, saw me through some of my toughest dark times. It's the best therapy in the world. My rescue pack fuel my quest to continue to help K9

Miracles around the world, the dogs who have lost all hope, but who finally reach loving homes for life.

Thanks to Rory Bremner for being so kind as to offer help, advice and tweeting my cause, and to all those lending their voices to those still suffering: Ricky Gervais, Peter Egan, Brian May, Dame Judi Dench, Marc Abraham, Will Young, Victoria Stilwell, Noel Fitzpatrick, and one man who had me glued to the TV from an early age engrossed in his wildlife programmes, Sir David Attenborough.

I'd like to thank the *Daily Mirror* for awarding Miracle 'Rescue Animal of the Year' at their 2015 Animal Hero Awards, where we were presented with his award by my favourite *Loose Woman*, the lovely Denise Welch; also to Anneka Svenska for filming a very special moment when we collected that award.

I'd like to thank Ciara Foley for the fabulous opportunity to put pen to paper, Tess and the Ebury team, and ghost writer Linda Watson-Brown for helping me put together the jigsaw of my life.

Last but by no means least – for the miracle that walked into my arms and life, who placed his paws on Scottish soil on 4/4/14 (World Stray Animals Day). Miracle is really no different to any other rescue but he is remembered and he is saving lives. You're adored King Miracle – this is just the beginning my boy!

Of course, there are many animals that have walked beside us too. The lifespan of an animal is never long enough but it has been a privilege to share time with so many amazing souls, all of them individuals in their own right. Thank you for being a part of life's journey – I hope someday to be surrounded by your love, licks and loyalty. I loved and lost you but I know you've never really left me.

Sleep tight: Beama, Khandi, Odin, Kamatz, Skeet, Cheeko, Freya, Jet, Troy, Kuzak, Bambi, Spirit, JC, EJ, No.1 and Smokey.